SOCCER SAMURAI

For Mags, with love and gratitude

SOCCER SAMURAI

A COUCH POTATO'S DIALECTICAL
DECONSTRUCTION OF WORLD CUP 2002

DAVID BENNIE

MAINSTREAM
PUBLISHING

EDINBURGH AND LONDON

First published in Great Britain in 2002 by
MAINSTREAM PUBLISHING COMPANY (EDINBURGH) LTD
7 Albany Street
Edinburgh EH1 3UG

ISBN 1 84018 654 2

A catalogue record for this book is available from the British Library

Typeset in Berkeley and Hammer
Printed and bound in Great Britain by
Mackays of Chatham

Acknowledgements

The author would like to thank Will Mackie at Mainstream for his editorial help in getting the text into publishable print, given some very tight turnaround deadlines.

Contents

Prologue: 'Hanoi, we have a problem'

Edinburgh, 30 May 2002

Four years after the Gallic *mise en scene* and French victory, the *caravanserai* associated with Planet Football's biggest moveable feast has rolled eastwards in order to set up its state-of-the-art 20-stadium infrastructure for the 17th World Cup. For the first time the competition is not being held in Europe or the Americas, but in Asia, with another innovation in the form of co-hosts – South Korea and Japan. Even the over-expanded Olympic Games are put in the sporting shade by the passionate heat and advertising light generated by football's world party, since soccer's cultural influence and popular appeal are almost literally global (and perhaps even universal if the late Carl Sagan was correct and extra-terrestrial intelligences are 'out there' and have been tuning in to radio broadcasts and television pictures ever since media coverage of the first tournament in 1930, when hosts Uruguay beat Argentina 4–2).[1]

Soccer is the *lingua franca* of humankind – certainly more so than the English language, Esperanto or mathematical formulae – and if its commercialisation is sad but inevitable, the footballisation of global consciousness is a continuing and welcome development (capable of subsuming creed, race or religion). It may not be as important as politics but it definitely provides more pleasure and causes less pain – although it has to be admitted that populist politicians and devious dictators have attempted to hijack the Beautiful Game for their own pernicious reasons. Football can be used not only to sell consumer products to the proletariat but to promote national, religious and racial divisions amongst the workers of the world (most of whom would rather give away their legal right to vote than lose their season tickets or their crystal-bucket television sets).

Bizarrely, only the USA has resisted football's cultural and commercial spread at club/city level – and even more ironically America's attempts to export its national game of baseball have only seen 'professional rounders' taking healthy root in Canada, Cuba, *South Korea* and *Japan*. Like cricket, however, baseball will always be a colonial-conquest minority-sport throwback, played by eccentric enthusiasts with two left feet. Soccer, or football, is in the sporting ascendant, with no other recreational ball game on the planet capable of competing with it on any proverbial level playing field – whether in terms of TV ratings, stadium attendances or numbers of people actually playing the game.

The controversial choice of co-hosts must have raised a few furry eyebrows amongst academic experts in the geopolitical history of the region. Dream-team twinnings involving, say, USA–Canada, Australia–New Zealand or Iceland–Faroe Islands could have been sold to FIFA's organising committee on the basis of 'a good socio-economic fit between friendly neighbours' (and Belgium–Holland successfully co-hosted Euro 2000), but even if not on an explosive par with such hackle-raising combinations as Israel–Palestine, India–Pakistan, Turkey–Greece or Eire–Northern Ireland, the Siamese conjoining of two historically antagonistic Asian tigers certainly poses potential diplomatic problems arising from the fact that Imperial Japan ruled Korea from 1910 to 1945 (during which period communicating in the Korean language was a capital crime). The mild-mannered Emperor Akihito was never invited to the opening ceremony in Seoul, in case his presence on South Korean soil resulted in rioting on the streets.

Japan remains one of the fortunate few nations that have never been invaded by an enemy army – although obviously it was occupied by the Americans after the official surrender following the nuclear bombing of Hiroshima and Nagasaki (neither of which were selected as host cities).[2] Prior to the attack on Pearl Harbour, Japan had already occupied much of China and taken from Russia the southern half of Sakhalin Island (which Soviet Russia later repossessed along with the disputed Kurile Islands). As a constitutional monarchy and capitalist democracy, Japan thrived economically after the Second World War, even with or maybe because of a Ground Self-Defence Force instead of an army, to the point where American corporations and congressmen feared a Japanese financial takeover of Hollywood, Silicon Valley and Wall Street in the form of leveraged buyouts (i.e. blue-chip shares and prime real estate being snapped up by inscrutable Oriental executives with suitcases full of yen and dollars, as when Sony purchased Columbia Pictures). Before Japan's economic bubble burst in the early '90s, its government was able to provide every town council with a million pounds for civic construction works, resulting in white-elephant opera houses and wooden footbridges being replaced by ferro-concrete flyovers.

Korea, on the other hand, is probably Asia's doormat equivalent of Poland – alongside Vietnam – when it comes to being invaded and occupied by nationalistic neighbours from hell. Before Japan, it suffered centuries of Chinese domination. After the Second World War, America occupied the south and Russia the north. Both superpowers withdrew after setting up puppet regimes in their own image, and war broke out in 1950 when the north invaded. General McArthur pushed the communists back and even captured their capital Pyongyang. China then entered the conflict and helped recapture the southern capital of Seoul. By 1951 the US and UN forces had pushed the communists back beyond the infamous 38th parallel, which divides Korea to this day.

So much for a back-of-the-envelope, potted history of the two host nations (an off-the-top-of-my-head description of an horrendously complicated past – with concomitant horrors and atrocities – which gives me a headache just trying to get straight in my sieve-and-sewer-like mind). And as for the history of China, Taiwan and Vietnam, and the roles played by ex-colonial powers like France, Britain, Belgium and Holland in the region, not to mention Russia and America . . . That would require a book-long history lesson, even a précis of which is beyond the complexity horizon of my mind's eye.

Suffice to say, South Korea are scheduled to play the United States, as well as playing host to France and China. Japan compete against Russia and Belgium, while accommodating England.

China are the only competing country categorisable as 'communist', although whether this fact will boost viewing figures in Cuba, Vietnam or North Korea is I suppose a moot point. Maybe being the sole red-flag-bearer vindicates Professor Fukiyama's thesis about *The End of History*. Communism as a workable economic and political system may have come crashing down with the Berlin Wall in 1989, with only the Soviet Union and Czechoslovakia ever succeeding in winning football silverware as communist countries (in the 1960 and 1976 European Championships respectively), but Russia as free-market footballers since 1991 have an appalling record in· international competition compared to their 'politically motivated' predecessors. But the future of football is unquestionably going to be directed by multinational movers and shakers rather than Marxist–Leninist apparatchiks. The Vietnamese Football Association Headquarters in Hanoi really do have a problem – their national squad will never emulate plucky fellow travellers North Korea, who in 1966 famously beat Italy to qualify for the quarter-finals, not unless their game at grass-roots level gets an injection of capitalist cash.

Fukiyama became a bestselling author and his hypothesis about the inevitable hegemony of capitalist democracy probably held theoretical water without leaking too obviously until the events of 11 September 2001, when 'the world changed forever'. After the Twin Towers of the World Trade Centre imploded hellwards towards Ground Zero, as shocking as the Pillars of Hercules being destroyed by bolts of vengeful lightning unleashed by mad minor deities on Mount Olympus, the ratings war between CNN and Al-Jazeera for the hearts and minds of slack-jawed viewers seemed to herald the start of another heavyweight ideological battle: between Christian–Judaic capitalism and Islamic–Arabian fundamentalism; smart bombs versus suicide bombers; high tech versus human sacrifice . . .

Hopefully terrorism will not raise one of its ugly Hydra heads at this World Cup – if it does one can only hope that the armed security guards are good enough marksmen to kill with a single head shot – but it will be interesting to see if the press and television coverage incorporates this new polarity of tribal allegiances. 'Surely not!' you may be silently screaming, but the media reporting at World Cups always takes into account actual and artificial differences between competing nations. In the past, the highlighted fault-line was that separating teams from Europe and South America. 'Eastern Bloc' can no longer be used to differentiate European countries, but the Nordic versus Latin dichotomy will be discussed in terms of 'disciplined' teams from north of the Alps, whereas countries bordering the Mediterranean will invariably be described as 'fiery in temperament'. Spanish-speaking countries from Central and South America are usually lumped together for purposes of 'in-depth analysis', in contrast to Portuguese-speaking multi-racial Brazil (the only country so far to win the tournament outside their 'home' continent – in Sweden in 1958).

The fact that this World Cup is being played in 'neutral' Asia, amidst soaring temperatures and high humidity, must surely favour the African nations (who Pelé in a blaze of publicity incorrectly predicted would provide world champions by the end of the 20th century). If capitalism versus socialism is an emotionally charged signification that no longer exists, will commentators and pundits be drawn to marking cultural cards with observations about the developed West competing against the developing South? Will the religious background of Tunisia and Saudi Arabia be a factor in the television coverage? Will Japan and South Korea suffer from stereotypical generalisations in the reporting of their cultures and matches?

South Korea–Japan 2002 will be this author's tenth experience of a World Cup, and like the previous nine any memorable messages that I receive will be filtered through the medium of television. In his book, *Understanding Media* (1964), Marshall McLuhan famously – and some would argue fatuously – observed that 'The medium is the message'. Ironically, after viewing all 64 matches on the 'hot' medium of television (so described because of its memorable visual impact and because if viewed simultaneously by millions of viewers it unites a human audience as part of a genuine global village), I will be disseminating my responses to and observations about the competition via the 'cold' medium of a printed book (so described because literature is consumed in isolation by relatively small numbers of readers and only becomes 'lukewarm' if sold in vast enough quantities to qualify for bestseller status and the accompanying television news coverage). Whether viewed on the BBC or ITV this World Cup will be a communal experience for a British audience because it is being broadcast on two terrestrial channels, as opposed to pay-per-view cable or subscription satellite. However, with early-morning and lunch-time kick-offs, the audiences in the UK will be significantly smaller than those for France '98 (or even compared to the viewing figures achieved during Argentina '78, when UK viewers only had to stay up late to catch live matches – a lot easier than getting up early!).

How the World Cup is presented in Britain by our two main rival terrestrial channels is not simply a matter of them both striving to show unmediated reality as honestly and objectively as their respective technologies, budgets and allocated air-times permit. Editorial decisions in boardroom meetings and directorial choices in production galleys will influence how viewers perceive what is happening – both during live fixtures and with off-the-pitch stories. For example, following games in one objective long-shot never happens, with some directors favouring constant close-ups of star players in man-marked action (not to mention excessive facial reaction close-ups that Steve McQueen would have killed to get from his movie directors). Live on-pitch action is also interrupted by video replays and even cut-away shots to 'atmospheric' Mexican Wave crowd scenes (never mind pornographer *manqué* camera operators zooming in on attractive young women with pendulous breasts and sweat-drenched T-shirts). God forbid that we get 'panoramic' shots of the stadiums taken from airships sponsored by Goodyear this time round. Developing stories involving argumentative, arrogant and oversexed millionaire players can either be 'killed' or allowed to run and run (with neither newspapers or television setting the agenda, but being led by each other). Each country of course interprets events from its own perspective, but even if England do well I hope the BBC remembers that there are 31 other teams in the World Cup.

Attending a World Cup in person – as a football fan, sports writer or football author – would be a dream come true, but at least for this one I have acquired a colour television for the first time in my life. Second-hand and 'on loan' it may be, but I'm looking forward to seeing all the matches in glorious technicolour. My working-class parents – *upper working-class* (sorry, Mum; and thanks for the loan of the 14-inch colour Akura portable TV!) – still had a black-and-white crystal-bucket during 1970's World Cup in Mexico, but I'll never forget my reaction as a wide-eyed nine-year-old when I saw the colour coverage of the Brazil–England game from Guadalajara on a proud neighbour's new status symbol Redifusion set. The grey-complexioned but red-faced English players kitted out in all-white *á la* Real Madrid looked like overweight extras in a late-1960s soap-powder commercial, but the olive-to-pitch-black-hued Brazilians stood out and ran around like exotic Aztec demi-gods bathed in Central American sunshine. At first sight, the bright yellow jerseys and light blue shorts were almost primary-colour painful to the eye, but I soon enjoyed not only the football but the aesthetically breathtaking colour combinations (which to a young boy brought up in the grey East End of Glasgow, and who was used to watching football highlights in various shades of grey, must have been like an adult collector replacing the paintings of L.S. Lowry and Francis Bacon with the multi-coloured work of David Hockney and Roy Lichtenstein).

Without Scotland to support (or snigger at in past-caring embarrassment) I have decided to adopt the suggestion of Scottish Nationalist MSP Andrew Wilson and give England my armchair backing. Wilson's rationale is based on the premise that if Scots were more self-confident they wouldn't feel psychologically/pathologically compelled to cheer on whoever England are up against on the football field. Indifference would at least be indicative of Scottish shoulders that weren't weighed down by century-old chips (or boulders), whereas *active* non-supporting of England supposedly betrays an adolescent national identity which is reduced to defining one's Scottishness solely and pathetically in terms of not being and not liking the English. In the past I have perhaps overcompensated for Scotland's absence from the latter stages of World Cups and non-appearance in European Championships by supporting England's opponents, but by so doing I was transforming myself from an impartial spectator back into a committed supporter (which may or may not have been mentally or morally healthy but which was without doubt a lot more *fun* – especially since England could be relied upon to self-destruct whenever they came within touching distance of their footballing Holy Grail: to win the World Cup again, but on foreign soil).

If a red-blooded male cannot *force* himself to find a woman devoid of any physical pulchritude sexually arousing, but can like and admire her as a morally decent human being, is there any way he could bring himself to satisfy her carnal desires (if he was the object of them)? Short of swallowing a handful of Viagra like Smarties, possibly not . . . But to reinforce my new commitment to England, I have just wagered £30 on Sven-Göran Eriksson's men to win the World Cup (at the less than generous odds of 9/1, I must say). The 30-quid stake was enough of a wallet-lightening sacrifice to hurt – and in the unlikely event of captain David Beckham lifting the trophy on the last day of June, £300 is the kind of monetary reward that would change my life for the better (at least in terms of being able to afford a holiday abroad for the first time since 1999, even if only a week on the Costa del Sol).

I reckon I'm half-way there already in my psychological quest to get my head around the concept of supporting England, since Scotland's failure to qualify for South Korea–Japan 2002 left me feeling apathetic in the extreme. In September of 2001 I only went along to Hampden to see if Scotland could secure a vital qualifying victory against Croatia because a ticket was procured on my behalf (without my knowledge and without any dropped hints from me indicating that I'd like to go). The 0–0 borefest summed up the current national team perfectly – possibly the least talented in the history of the Scottish game and definitely one of the most boring and predictable currently playing on the international football stage. When France humbled the new Scottish coach Bertie Vögts by beating his 'experimental' team 5–0 in a World Cup warm-up game in the Stade de France in April, I simply enjoyed the free-flowing football played by the French and relished the unstoppably brilliant nature of their trademark goals.

World Cup 2002 kicks off in just over 12 hours' time and I'm hoping it will help rekindle my enthusiasm for the Beautiful Game. My memories of Mexico, Germany, Argentina, Spain, Mexico (again), Italy, America and even France '98 are all indelible (and largely positive). Scottish club football provides no personal pleasure anymore, nor even piques any real interest, and with the exceptions of a Falkirk versus Berwick Rangers Scottish Cup third-round replay in 2000 and the aforementioned Scotland game last year, a Celtic–St Johnstone League decider on the last day of season 1997–98 remains the last game I attended in person of my own excited volition.

Watching football on television while sitting on a sofa or armchair is more typical of the modern football fan's experience than actually sitting down in a stadium and cheering on a team in person. The experience is neither better nor worse – simply different. It's cheaper and more comfortable, if somewhat removed from the electrically charged atmospheres that can provide medically measurable adrenaline highs to those in attendance. Watching on TV you can suffer the ennui of merely spectating passively, whereas when sitting in a stand identifying strongly with one team, you are an excited supporter losing yourself in the human drama being played out on the pitch.

Roll on France versus Senegal, even if I only have seven weeks to write up 64 matches played over a single month. Previously I had five months to encapsulate a lifetime of supporting Glasgow Celtic (a hardback which went into an updated paperback but both of which are now permanently out of print). A year spent visiting every Scottish League ground obviously took a year to write (and although the hardback is still technically in print, it never progressed anywhere near the sales level that would have justified paperback publication – and never will, since apart from anything else it is now horribly out of date). Still, this time I'm not writing and having to hold down day-jobs simultaneously (although if my 'sabbatical' costs me promotion to either check-out captain or head trolley boy from my old position as supermarket shelf-replenisher I'm going to be very, very disappointed). The sacrifices we artists and writers have to make for our art, eh?

Come on, En-gur-land! Get stuck intae – sorry, into – them Swedes/Argies/Nige– Eagles, mate, Eagles!

NOTES
[1] If the radio waves emitted by television transmissions have been broadcasting from Planet Earth for approximately 50 years, does that mean for half a century TV programming has been sent out into space in all directions at the *speed of light*? And if so, could ETs on, say, Alpha Centauri, just now be picking up the 1970 World Cup final on their electromagnetic-spectrum analysers? What idea would they get about the human race from

our crystal-bucket art? In soap-operas for example, less than five per cent of sexual activity between men and women takes place between married couples. What if ETs are basing their judgements on a single channel like ITV1 – or even Channel 5? Being something of a closet intellectual, or selective viewer at least, ITV1 and BBC1 could stop transmitting and I wouldn't realise for days on end (since I only tune in occasionally for sport and movies). The original of this endnote took me a full day to write using a fountain pen, consisting as it did of quite an amusing riff on this theme of appalled ETs watching human telly (a piece of fine writing that ran for six sodding pages), but I've inadvertently shredded all the handwritten pages. Fuck! . . . (Not to mention the chaos I've created so far on a borrowed laptop typing in all of the above.) In my mind, all these lost Notes for this Prologue have become the best written pages in the whole damn book. I'm so angry and frustrated I'm going to stop after the second note, with no attempt to recreate Notes 3 or 4 . . . If I had a cat I'd drop-kick the meowing little irritation right out of the kitchen window if it came anywhere near me at the moment. All that work wasted! I'm casting around in my fit-to-burst mind for someone else to blame – and if I have to speak to someone in person in the next hour I'm going to give whoever calls a mouthful of abuse (I just know it). 'Transference? Sign up for an anger-management course? Me? Don't talk such bloody offensive nonsense, okay! Rewrite it? For fuck's sake, it was hard enough the first time around. Sir Walter who? Scott? Rewrote a lost MS on the history of the French Revolution by just sitting down and starting from scratch, did he? What's admirable about that? That's just sick, if you ask me . . . Positively perverse. You tell that anecdote as if it reflects well on him as a human being. It betrays a lack of ordinary human feeling, of head-banging frustration, that would have been the normal reaction from anyone except that old duffer. Hey, wait, I remember now: his maid burnt the MS by mistake, didn't she? Well, he should have whacked her over the head with a fire-poker. Don't tell me to fucking calm down . . .' 'Just rewrite as best you can.' Christ... C-Drive. Fuck, I don't believe this. Where's A-Drive? AAAArrrrrrgggghhhhhhhhhhhhhhhhhhhhh!!!!!!!!!!!!!!!!!!!!!!!!!!!!!!!!!!!!!!!

[2] The morality of dropping nuclear bombs on Japan is an issue I've never been able to decide on one way or another. Even if the detonations over civilian cities did help to save many American lives – even more than the numbers who died in Hiroshima and Nagasaki – the deployment of nuclear

weapons is a fact that the USA can never wipe from the history books. On the other hand, Japan was an Axis power with an appalling human-rights record during the war, and if I had been in President Harry S. Truman's place I may well have sanctioned the use of atomic weapons to bring about an end to the conflict, rather than permit tens of thousands of young American servicemen to die in a war of attrition battling to take Japanese island after Japanese island, with hand-to-hand fighting all the way to Tokyo. Whether *two* bombs were absolutely necessary to make the point that Japan should surrender unconditionally, and whether they should have been dropped on civilian cities rather than military bases, are questions that can be legitimately raised with moral hindsight, but I'm just glad I wasn't the chief executive making the decision or either of the bombardiers responsible for unleashing 'Fat Man' or 'Little Boy'.

1. What's French for *Va Va Merde*?

France 0 Senegal 1
Seoul: Friday, 31 May, 12.30 p.m., ITV

As in the opening match of Italia '90, when Cameroon embarrassed Argentina thanks to one Oman Biyick, this World Cup kicked off with an *ancien regime* being overthrown by a single goal scored by African underdogs '*sans culottes*'. Apparently £5.5 million was spent on the usual 'spectacular' opening ceremony, boring an estimated 2.5 billion human beings across the globe glued to their crystal buckets, but those who managed to stay awake for the football which followed had their eyes well and truly opened. Senegal never really looked like losing after Papa Bouba Diop tapped home the winner within half an hour. Superstar-in-the-making El Hadj Diouf skinned Frank '*Vous est le weakest link*' Lebouef on the left before delivering a fairly innocuous cross that Emmanuel Petit and Fabien Barthez somehow contrived to make fatal. The French midfielder tried to clear for an unnecessary corner but Barthez sprang into action like a circus clown high on cannabis (the smoking of which earned him a four-month ban in 1996). He inexplicably prevented the corner at the expense of setting up Diop, who celebrated by dancing around his discarded shirt with his smiling team-mates by the far corner flag.

Commentator Clive Tyldsley refrained from making any wisecracks about tribal dancing, having already mentioned 'witch doctors' as early as the 14th minute. To be fair to the professional and personable successor to ITV's Brian Moore, he only brought up the subject when quoting African Footballer of the Year Diouf's excuse for being late in returning to club training at Lens after helping Senegal to reach the recent African Nations Cup Final (where his country only missed out on penalties to Cameroon). Diouf may prove to be 'difficult to handle' on Merseyside, having signed for Liverpool immediately after this game, but consulting witch doctors – or Mouribe holy men to be exact, Clive – is no more ridiculous or irrational than Western yuppies paying for '50-minute hours' of spiritual guidance from psychotherapists, feng shui consultants or life coaches; plus, it's undoubtedly a damn sight less expensive and probably a lot more effective.

Co-commentator Ron Atkinson contributed another priceless example of his version of 'Colemanballs' – 'Ron-glish' – describing a French forward as having a penchant for taking 'a *blatter* at free-kicks' (which sadly wasn't a sly dig at Sepp Blatter, the recently re-elected president of FIFA who was facing charges of financial corruption that would have embarrassed Nixon into resigning, even if Richard Milhous Nixon *was* a great man brought down by political pygmies). Now that ITV's production team have made explanations of Ron-glish into a regular feature – the first translating 'lollipops' into *step-overs* – you can only hope that Big Ron isn't tempted into making non-genuine neologisms, because they would inevitably lose their innocent charm for those of us who believe the English language is fluid and evolving (unlike the anal French with their Academy to police the 'purity' of their mother tongue).

One of the few French successes on the pitch was Arsenal's Thierry Henry, who hit the Senegalese crossbar, and the multi-lingual millionaire appeared as the new face of Renault's advertising campaign for the Clio super-mini during the half-time commercial breaks (of which there were two in fifteen minutes, ITV cramming in a total of sixteen separate commercials). Henry was chosen to follow in the high-heeled footsteps of actresses Estelle 'Papa!' Skornik and Helene 'Size matters' Mahieu, whose appearances in these award-winning and long-running adverts earned them both small fortunes and official fan clubs in the UK, although still no successful film careers as I write. (Needless to say, real fucking life is nothing like the representation of human existence as sold to us opinion-following suckers in glossy car commercials; even ads for household cleaning products have a *Truman Show*-esque unreality about them.)

Henry came across as attractive, stylish and articulate, delivering his punchline slogan – 'What is French for *Va Va Voom*?' – with charismatic aplomb. Disappointingly the Glasgow Rangers manager/coach Alex McLeish didn't come across quite so charismatically in his front-man role for the Rangers Direct commercial which was broadcast after the final whistle (although personally I blame the director – Alan Smithee? – for dressing him in a blazer, striped tie and polyester slacks, as well as having his star pointing at the camera like a wooden Lord Kitchener trying to recruit foot soldiers for a pyramid-selling scam).[1]

Along with the starting 11s of Italy, Spain, Germany, England, Brazil and Argentina, France are a team made up exclusively of sporting millionaires. France's much-vaunted multi-cultural, multi-racial stars play abroad in the licence-to-print-money leagues of England, Spain, Italy and Germany (with the obvious exception of lumbering Lebouef, who Chelsea managed to offload to Olympic Marseille), whereas most of the Senegalese squad earn enough money to send some home to relatives by playing for poor provincial French clubs.

Senegal was a French colony until independence in 1960, even if Paul Gascoigne had 'never heard of Senegal' until turning up to do a turn with straight man Terry Venables as part of ITV's opening-day lunchtime panel. With at least one arched eyebrow, and possibly an O Level in Geography, Des Lynam wryly observed that 'It's been part of Africa for quite some time now, Paul'. Thankfully Gazza didn't reply: 'Africa? Where's that, Des – south of the Tyne? Which is all mine, pet!' It used to be part of French West Africa, of course, which must be where the Geordie geographer's confusion arose from.

Honestly, the way these ex-colonies chop and change their names at the drop of a pith helmet is very confusing and irritating. Even as a liberal humanist, I found the rapid 'Zaire-isation' of the Belgian Congo after the Fleming and Walloon colonisers pulled out in 1973 a bit of a slap in the face – although that's undoubtedly an unforgivable Eurocentric example of cultural absolutism. (Seriously, however, two days later a tabloid headline informed its readership that Gazza had just had a brain scan and even if he isn't suffering from brain damage I hope his agent keeps him off these pundit-on-a-panel gigs, because the poor man is drowning not waving in any semi-serious attempt at football analysis).

During the three minutes of extra-time, as France pushed

frenetically for a face-saving equaliser, I finally figured out my supporting allegiance – coming down with a decisive thud on the side of the Senegalese. An early exit for France would have been a major disappointment for all fair-minded admirers of their footballing flair, but Frenchman Bruno Metsu's men fully deserved 15 minutes of footballing fame for their exciting yet disciplined performance. And as an added bonus this result will probably have stuck in the craw of politicians like Jean-Marie Le Pen, with an admittedly multi-ethnic *Les Bleus* well beaten by an unknown collection of 'immigrant Africans'.

Le Pen's 'shock' success in reaching the presidential play-offs of 2002 actually owed more to an anachronistic system of democracy in which multiple left-wing candidates split the vote and shot socialist candidate Lionel Jospin in both knee-caps than to any statistically significant surge to the far right. But if a disenchanted electorate 'protest votes' for such a dubious demagogue, they can hardly complain when they wake up in the morning to find that he has secured a platform on which to broadcast his hidden agenda of racist discrimination.

In the two-horse race between Jacques Chirac (allegedly 'a crook') and Le Pen (undoubtedly 'a Fascist'), the unacceptable face of French politics secured less than 20 per cent of the vote, so at least there was no repeat of 1848's disaster for democracy when Charles Louis Napoleon Bonaparte was put up as a 'beard' or joke candidate and actually beat his Jospin-equivalent opponent Cavaignac by four million votes! Hence the election of Napoleon Bonaparte's gadfly grandson to the presidency, followed by 25 long years during which he systematically restricted democratic liberties and commissioned Haussmann to raze old Paris to the ground in order to rebuild with wide boulevards capable of being riot-policed by charging cavalry. Lunatic Louis inspired the first recorded use of a bomb as a political protest weapon (even if the first group of three devices thrown at him missed, killing eight fellow opera-goers instead).

The French Revolution itself was typically flawed French democracy in action, with more style than content, orchestrated by the middle classes to satisfy their base bourgeois desires for a greater share of aristocratic money, position and prestige. It had of course to be justified with hypocritical, high-sounding rhetoric as knitting fishwives clicked and clucked with delight as wicker baskets filled with the decapitated heads of high-living aristocrats. The original Napoleon took up the mantle of 'people's Emperor' and used a spin-doctoring plebiscite to confer credibility upon his dictatorial position (and Napoleon is now only a suitable name for a snorting pig).

A massive government bureaucracy was formed to meet the materialistic wants of the middle-classes, and it provided salaried sinecures with pensions, along with flattering uniforms and a cornucopia of shiny medals for pinning on puffed-out chests. The Legion of Honour roll-call of the great and the good exists to this supposedly egalitarian day and has about as much to do with the concept of liberty, equality and fraternity as *Who's Who*, *Debrett's Guide to Debutantes* or the *New York Social Register*. Pompous but honest President Daladier admitted as much when he observed that France has been run by a mere 200 families since the Revolution.

Algerian-born Zinedine Zidane missed his side's humiliation because of a pulled hamstring, and it's hard to believe that during my lifetime the French human-rights record in trying to hold on to this particular ex-colony was so bad that it makes ex-paratrooper Le Pen seem like an altruistic internationalist today. The notorious OAS (Secret Army Organisation) accepted deserters from the Foreign Legion and waged a brutal and bloody war against inevitable independence that included machine gunning burqua-wearing Arab women in the streets of Oran and Algiers, and which almost toppled the French Republic led by General Charles de Gaulle. Senegal didn't suffer like Algeria, which achieved independence two years and many lost lives later (and in 2002 Senegal actually knocked out Morocco *and* Algeria from their World Cup qualifying group). It may be worth noting that eight out of ten of the world's poorest countries are governed by various transplanted and updated versions of the *Code Napoleon*.

I have just realised that I will never now join the Foreign Legion – even if the idea is no more than a depressive's daydream – because I am 41 years old and the romantic regiment of Beau Geste & Co. has recently introduced a cut-off age of 40 for would-be recruits (as well as politically correct computer checks for serious criminal offences, to be followed soon no doubt by national insurance numbers, E111 health-care certificates and at least an A Level in French as entrance requirements).

Technically too old for the Foreign Legion.[2] *Merde!* Still, I could always lie about my age or even sign up in the name of '*Monsieur Frank Lebouef*'[3]

'*Non, mon Capitâine. C'est un nom de plume . . . Oof! Pardon . . . Nom de guerre, oui . . . Je demandez to voir la representative de la embassy de Ecossais! Ouch! Je vouloir –* sniff *– ma mere. Aagh . . . Mama!*'

NOTES

[1] The half-time commercials were broadcast in the following brand-name order: (first batch) Adidas, Budweiser, Michelin, Cirio, Adidas, Tango, Adidas, Health Education Board for Scotland (HEBS); (second batch) Tennents, Renault, Microsoft, McDonalds, Nike, T. Mobile, Lynx and Tennents.

The generic products being sold to increase the happiness of consumers with disposable income were: sportswear, beer, tyres, pasta sauce, sportswear, soft drink, sportswear, *celibacy*; lager, cars, computer services, fast food, sportswear, mobile phones, deodorant and lager.

The commercial breaks were top-'n'-tailed by programme sponsorship inserts for Travelex foreign exchange (a desperate and limited selection of World Cup 'highlights' from previous competitions which will undoubtedly become so irritating by the end of this World Cup that the company will be generating negative goodwill in exchange for name recognition amongst most ITV viewers).

England head coach Sven-Göran Eriksson was promoting an Italian pasta sauce that I had never heard of – the above Cirio – and he had signed up with promoters IMG to maximise his potential earnings, a deal that included endorsing everything from Sainsbury's supermarkets to PlayStation games. Various England players had been recruited to feature in ads for McDonalds, including Teddy Sheringham and Rio Ferdinand. Andre Agassi popped up extolling the benefits of keeping in touch with wife Steffi via a mobile-phone network. Following the full-time whistle, Michael Owen appeared guzzling Lucozade (which when I was his age was regarded as a glucose health drink for housebound or hospitalised invalids, and came in a glass bottle wrapped in orange cellophane, but which has since been successfully rebranded as an energy drink in plastic containers for professional sportsmen and busy professional young executives).

The hilarious HEBS infomercial is worthy of comment for two reasons. Firstly, even if only broadcast in Scotland thanks to digital technology, the cost of buying this airtime half-way through the World Cup's opening fixture must have been well-nigh prohibitive for a publicly-funded quango (I would have thought). Secondly, the content of this health-education/public-information film amounted to public moralising with no health message whatsoever. The other five films in the HEBS portfolio actually warn against the dangers of drug-taking, underage drinking, smoking and unprotected sex. Even the popular 'Stinx' film – with the catchy theme tune which hit the Scottish charts – makes the (dubious) point that teenage girls who smoke run the (ridiculous!) risk of turning teenage boys (or subtextual sugar-daddies?) off them sexually (yeah, right); but the one they chose to broadcast – 'His/Her Story' – had me scratching my crotch in confusion when I first saw it. Two teenagers have a one-night, or one-hour, stand at a party and from both 'povs' (filmspeak for points-of-view, don't ya know) they regret it since both are frowningly worried that they have lost the respect of their respective 'lovers' (Jeezuz!). It doesn't draw audience attention to any lack of contraception or the risk of catching an STD; it simply implies/states that promiscuous sex with strangers is morally wrong and will make you feel bad afterwards (even if you are over the age of consent and your hormones are raging).

So just say no, kids, okay? Hmm . . .

Sex education is one thing, 'moral majority' hectoring quite another.

As I write, the naffest commercial I have ever seen (including those for local Indian restaurants shown in fleapit cinemas) is running on my *colour* TV (and I still haven't got over the novelty value of seeing football played on a bright green pitch rather than a murky grey one). Promoting the Glasgow *Evening Times* as *the* newspaper for in-depth coverage and expert analysis of the World Cup, it stars two talking *socks*, each kitted out with a scarf from either side of the sectarian Old Firm divide. And no, the background wasn't bluescreen with computer-generated special effects; it was a hand-painted pantomime backdrop of the old Stirling Library with the equestrian statue out front topped with a traffic bollard (which in the Big G passes for funny slapstick visual humour). I can't help but wonder if the hands up the socks belong to an Equity actor or a professional puppeteer? What fee did the human being involved in 'animating' the socks receive? Did he also do the voices? Tuppence would be two pence too much if you ask me.

Sometimes it's really embarrassing being Scottish *and* Glaswegian.

[2] Hey, so what if I'm too old for the Foreign Legion and am writing about this World Cup from the cold comfort of my crummy apartment instead of an air-conditioned love hotel in downtown Tokyo? After all, the French writer Xavier de Maistre wrote *A Journey Round My Bedroom* without leaving its confines. It was published and became a bestseller (but only in Paris).

[3] 'Soccer Star to Shelf Stacker: X in Safeway Job' by John Bynorth (*The Scottish Sun*, 31 May 2002, pages 1, 2, 3 and 8).

Whatever fate befalls Leboeuf after he retires from the game, he definitely won't end up being humiliated by a tabloid exposing his shameful descent to the level of a shelf-stacker in a supermarket. Sacked by his club last year for alleged cocaine-snorting in a nightclub, the former £1,000-a-week Premier League striker was caught by a *Sun* snapper during his first night shift. The 'exclusive' managed to get in a dig about scoring with white powder (in the form of washing powder) – which was the only imaginative or well-written paragraph in the whole tawdry piece. The usual unidentified 'insider' remarked on the star's decline, along with always anonymous colleagues. Zoom lens photos pictured his £5.60-per-hour predicament, as well as capturing his reaction to being 'doorstepped' in his dressing gown. An unsigned editorial – 'Welcome to the real world' – pretended to praise him for his lack of self-pity and determination to work, but between the lines crowed with pleasure at highlighting his downfall. 'This is how they live, X, the good people . . .who once cheered you at –.' Maybe, but it's not how your average tabloid 'investigative reporter' makes ends meet, is it?

From my own personal experience, I know that 'shelf-replenishing' over a nine-hour shift is bloody hard yakker, quite incredibly boring and extremely poorly paid. My worst moment involved an acquaintance walking down the aisle and spotting me in my colourful company uniform. 'Bit of a comedown this, eh?' he cheerfully remarked. If the positions had been reversed I'd have taken *schadenfreudistic* pleasure in his humiliation, I must admit, but I wouldn't have said what he did. I thought about punching his lights out, but decided against it – shelf replenishers can be summarily dismissed for hitting customers no matter how cheeky or annoying or offensive (yet another disadvantage of this kind of job – which in places like Paris or London wouldn't be filled if not for the willingness of foreign immigrants to take any menial work they can get).

2. Are You Watching, Roy Keane?

Republic of Ireland I Cameroon I
Niigata: Saturday, I June, 7.30 a.m., BBC

Civil wars are notoriously more vicious than battles waged against external enemies, as in the historical cases of Ireland and Yorkshire, so that when the good-craic-and-cold-Guiness bonhomie of the Irish squad was ripped asunder by an outbreak of internecine conflict, it was time to declare that no personal prisoners would be taken. When Roy 'I bleed green' Keane exploded at Barnsley-born coach Mick 'Plastic Paddy' McCarthy for a reported six minutes of effing-and-ceeing verbal vitriol, it was reminiscent of King Rauidrhi O'Connor squaring up to Henry II of England. As George Bernard Shaw said, 'Put an Irishman on the spit and you can always get another to turn him.'

Keane was Ireland's one world-class player, a dedicated professional with a Nietzschian will-to-power when it comes to winning (on the pitch or in person). When he aggressively eyeballed the gruffly avuncular Irish manager in full view of the squad, the proverbial Unstoppable Force (Keane) was about to come into explosive contact with the proverbial Immovable Object (McCarthy). Ego tried to stare down Pride and Pride stared straight back without blinking.

The result? Keane on the first flight home to Cheshire (the favoured country suburb of Manchester for commuting to and from Old Trafford). A taciturn and thin-lipped Keane was filmed walking along leafy lanes with his attack-trained best friend (his brute of a dog). All over the Republic families divided in support of either their 'brave' star player or their 'decisive' team coach, with a wailing and gnashing of teeth not heard since the first potato famine. Who the hell was the hero of the hour, however, and who the feck was the villain of the piece? Without clear fault lines being drawn by a confused media, how could tea and sympathy be offered to the blameless victim and brickbats and condemnation administered to the guilty party?

'Jay-sus, what the feck's going on?' Irish football fans must have wondered, since this was the kind of self-destructive behaviour more associated with their Scottish cousins on World Cup duty.

What was the argument about and what was said exactly and by whom? Apparently Keane had gone on record and into print complaining about amateurish training facilities and McCarthy had confronted him with the offending article in front of all the other players. Keane shouldn't have criticised team management *publicly* and McCarthy shouldn't have demanded an explanation in a personal confrontation in front of the whole squad. I think we can be certain that Keane hadn't been quoted in the Irish press criticising his boss's Gaelic, resulting in the following fantasy exchange:

McCarthy: 'I am the Irish Coach and am therefore above grammar.'

Keane: 'An Irish gentleman need not know Gaelic, but he should at least have forgotten it!'

In football, as elsewhere in life, exceptional talent demands a certain amount of leeway when it comes to enforcing standards of acceptable behaviour, but a line does have to be drawn somewhere if authority is not going to descend into anarchy. For example, if spare-tire-sporting and short-of-speed central defender Richard Dunne of Manchester City had raised his voice, sworn like a trouper and blown a loud raspberry at his manager, he could have expected punishment in the form of a fine, whereas Manchester United match-winner Keane would reasonably have expected to get away with such a display (especially if he grudgingly apologised later). Rules are rules, but some of us can bend them more than others because of our powerful influence. But when you snap one across your knee in front of an authority figure and verbally taunt your official superior, with fellow 'slaves' witnessing the confrontational scene, it's asking for a Spartacus scenario to be set into motion (but Keane's team-mates weren't exactly jumping up and down in front of the frenzied media shouting: 'No, I'm Spartacus!').

Keane the moody loner and moaning prima donna was interviewed back in the UK on the Manchester United cable channel, an exercise that smacked of PR damage limitation directed at an audience across the Irish Sea. Even at this point a stage-managed, gritted-teeth, faked-sincerity 'apology' to McCarthy would have left the door ajar for Keane's return to Japan. He chose not to make one, no doubt sincerely believing he was in the moral right, but in years to come Keane will undoubtedly wish he had offered to crawl naked over hot coals in order to have regained his place in the Irish starting 11. Even if he does now regret letting down his team-mates and Irish supporters – bitterly, to the point of window-pane smashing with a frustrated fist – there is no way he is going to admit as much, not even on his death-bed as on old man with a priest hovering in the bedroom shadows. Emotions are not skilled workers and you can be sure that in his mind and memory Keane will *never* forgive McCarthy for depriving him of his last shot at World Cup glory (since Keane is 30 and Eire are by no means expected to qualify for the German World Cup in 2006). Whether Ireland won the World Cup in Japan or failed to gain a point from their group games, Keane was in a psychological and PR no-win situation. McCarthy on the other hand had one get-out-of-jail-free card up his sleeve: a degree of success, or even honourable failure, in the absence of his high-tailing-it-outta-here-no-show captain.

Cameroon may not be footballing giants but they are no soccer pygmies and they awaited a weakened Ireland team in the blazing sunshine of the Big Swan Stadium, having wisely decided or been forced to dispense with the basketball vests they had been playing in, in favour of a sartorial return to football jerseys with short sleeves. They have been the best team to come out of Africa for the past 20 years and set about dismantling McCarthy's shellshocked makeshift-and-make-do journeymen with attacking vengeance. A single Mboma goal was all that separated the teams at half-time, however, and Eire's only hopeful sign was the strength-saving shadow creeping across the pitch. McCarthy, in T-shirt and shorts, looked hot and bothered on the touchline; Cameroon's German coach Winifried Schafer, in lounge suit and thin tie, appeared cool and content (even with a fright-wig of long blonde hippyesque hair).

In the remarkable second half, left-back Ian Harte lost possession like a nervous schoolboy, allowing Real Madrid's Geremi Fotso the formality of sealing Ireland's losers' fate. The 23-year-old screwed his shot past Shay Given's far post. In the highlights package at night I'm surprised the words 'PIVOTAL MOMENT' weren't flashed up in big red letters a foot high.

If character is destiny, Mick McCarthy really does owe Geremi a few pints of the dark stuff in a Dublin bar, because this dreadful miss swung the footballing fates in favour of the toiling Irish. If the ball had gone in, McCarthy would have been buried by the Emerald Isle press corps; instead they would be coming to his post-match press conference to praise him. His staunch bhoys promptly went up the park and scored a terrific goal. Roy Keane's replacement, Matt Holland of Ipswich Town, hit a low and unstoppable 30-yarder (a ten-out-of-ten impression of a typical Roy Keane goal). The 7,000-odd Irish fans in attendance soon broke out into singing chants of: 'Are you watching, Roy Keane?' If he was he couldn't have failed to experience mixed emotions. His namesake, Robbie Keane, even hit the post before the end.

If Geremi had scored and opened the floodgates, McCarthy would have been about as popular as Pope Hadrian I, the only English pontiff in Vatican history, who attempted to gift Ireland to the English crown. But he didn't score and on this occasion history didn't choose to take the long way to Tipperary...

I was happy with the fairness of a draw and if I ever emigrate I definitely fancy the Republic over Cameroon (and not just because I'm not one-eighth Cameroonian). Any country that gives tax exemption to writers can't be all bad, although I get this benefit in Britain (but only when my annual earnings dip below the tax threshold, which is one definition of grinding but genteel poverty). At least McCarthy won't have to share the fate of one of my favourite Marxists, Dr Felix Moumie, who tried to organise a communist insurrection in Cameroon from the tax haven of Switzerland. On his death-bed in 1960, his last words claimed that he had been poisoned by a secret organisation called 'The Red Hand'. Maybe he died before he could get the rest of the description finished: '. . . of Ul . . . Uls . . . Uls . . . Aaaahh.' Ulster, Ullswater or Ulsan?

I hope that one day Roy Keane and Mick McCarthy will shake hands and make up. But they never will. Because people who hate each other never do, do they?[1]

NOTES

[1] There are only two human beings in this world who I actually personally *hate*. It's not a good feeling to have, I can tell you, but since both are functionally illiterate and never read books, they're hardly likely to read this. I could hit both *Das Suppenlöffel* and *Das Siamkatze* hard and more than once, but hopefully I'll never feel compelled to seek them out to do so. Two is two too many, of course, but if I'm honest it's an underestimate by two-thirds.

As for people I actively dislike and would like to hurt with a few well-chosen words, there's probably a mental blacklist of about half-a-dozen, with *Das Dampfmaschine* near the top. What's the point in keeping your youthful figure if your face has collapsed to the point of physical repellence? And if you should ever read this post-publication, I hope you're blushing to the roots of your dry, dyed hair. Come to think of it, you're definitely in the previous category

3. The Latin Swiss Versus the Euro Brazilians

Uruguay 1 Denmark 2
Ulsan: Saturday, 1 June, 10 a.m., ITV

Uruguay famously won the first two World Cups they entered, but surprisingly were semi-finalists as recently as 1970. A major exporter of beef, Uruguay actually has a city called Fray Bentos (an evocative name for those of us who, while living in bed-sits, would open a can before shoving it in the mini-oven of a Baby Belling portable cooker). Like most of its neighbours, it has been at war with Paraguay, but only for an insignificant six years in total (hence its nickname of the Switzerland of South America). Denmark used to export raping and pillaging Vikings, diversified into pornography and now sends skilful footballers all over Europe. They like to boast of being the European Brazil, a somewhat dubious claim despite having won the European Championships of 1992 in Sweden (as late call-up replacements for disintegrating Yugoslavia).

The first half consisted of Denmark's brand of 'liquid football' against free-kicks taken exclusively by Alvaro Recoba of Inter Milan (who reputedly pay their Uruguayan star £5 million a season). The Danes do play with *three* up front and *two* wingers, an attacking formation that must have given Uruguay coach Victor Pua a migraine behind his dark glasses. Known to his face as 'The Fat Man' he is the spitting image of Sidney Greenstreet in *Casablanca*. Danish midfield bull Stig Tofting of Bolton Wanderers reminded me of R2D2 in *Star Wars*, and apparently he does occasionally go charging off course into big trouble. John Dahl Tomasson side-footed a deserved opener.

Just after the restart, ITV viewers were treated to an early nominee for best goal of the tournament. Pablo Garcia chested down a bouncing ball just outside Denmark's 'D', kneed it up and hit a square floating pass to his left. Full-back Dario Rodriguez arrived at pace and hit a left-foot volley from a computer-measured '24 yards', the ball travelling at '77.33 mph' into the top left-hand corner. With no Peter Schmeichel in goal this tournament, the thunderstruck Danish defenders weren't subjected to high-decibel deprecations that could have deafened them for life. Near the end Feyenoord's Tomasson rose unmarked but gracefully to head the winner.

Pointless France versus pointless Uruguay five days later had 'fun and games' written all over it . . .

4. Sand-dancing in Sapporo

Germany 8 Saudi Arabia 0
Sapporo: Saturday, 1 June, 12.30 p.m., BBC

The first of September 2001 would be totally superseded in the world's collective consciousness ten days later (courtesy of a handful of suicidal Saudis and other Arab nationals), but I clearly recall settling down in complacent expectation to watch England getting turned over in the *Olympiastadion München* (after having left Hampden Park earlier in the day with a heavy heart, a sluggish Scotland having drawn that miserable blank against an ageing but coasting-to-qualification Croatia). The Germans took a predictable lead, but after rubbing my hands together in complacent expectation very strange things began to happen in front of my rapidly blinking, disbelieving eyes (as if the footballing equivalent of the laws of nature had been rewritten from the perspective of Einsteinian quantum physics and redrafted in the form of Erikssonian string theory, with black holes opening up in the space/time continuum of the German defence and God playing dice with the England forward line's shooting boots). 'Deutschland 1, Engerland 5' still won't be believed on Alpha Centauri when the time-delayed radio waves finally reach there ('Listen, mate, give that spectrum analyser a good thump with your tail, because it's broadcasting the most unbelievable rubbish in amongst the static!'). Planet Football rocked on its axis and I hadn't felt that emotionally gutted since watching in despair as Manchester United snatched the European Cup from Bayern Munich in 1999 with two late, late goals (proving if nothing else that televised football fixtures still had the psychological potential to affect me physiologically – i.e. make me feel physically sick – even if not in the direction of light-headed elation).

I felt a similar sense of stomach-dropping unreality on 11

September 2001, but multiplied dramatically, when I realised that the black-and-white afternoon matinee on Channel 4 had not been replaced by a modern made-for-TV disaster movie (a realisation that didn't completely take over until the second plane had crashed and the first tower had collapsed).

Despite obvious security concerns, the World Cup was up and safely running. When Germany and Saudi Arabia walked out under the cover of the Sapporo Dome, no one watching expected that the current holders of the Gulf Cup and scorers of 47 goals in qualifying would give their opponents anything less than a highly competitive 90 minutes. The avalanche of German goals took all of 20 minutes to start, with five of the eight successes coming from high Teutonic foreheads. The Aryans positively towered over their Arab counterparts, who threw in the beach towel as early as the third goal. In the commentary, a princely supporter in the stands was described as wearing a 'turban' for Chrissakes, and although 'towel-head' would have been unacceptable on the BBC it would at least have been more accurate. The red-and-white garment worn by male members of the Saudi royal family is a kind of Arab head-dress, not a bloody turban! The woman next to this character was wearing a full burkha, topped with a natty baseball cap. If she was a real soccer fan, really willing on her national team, she must have wished that the eyeholes were covered by an *opaque* veil.

I felt little sympathy for the short-arsed, sand-dancing Saudis, remembering how their 'Under-16' youth team had beaten their fellow finalists at Hampden in 1989. That genuinely had been a case of men against boys, five-o'clock shadows and 6 ft physiques betraying a squad of players of indeterminate age, whereas all the Scots were still at school (even if signed on S-forms to professional clubs).

The Saudi's Al-Deayea played in tracksuit bottoms, which I always interpret as a bad sartorial sign amongst that self-confessed crazy gang of specialist footballers called goalkeepers. But even with a world-class keeper the Saudis would still have been hit for six or so, with Polish-born Miroslav Klose probably still grabbing a hat-trick with three headed goals.

Rudi Völler looked pleased with eight, but his coaching counterpart Nasser Al-Johar spent the last few minutes flicking through the A4 pages of his clipboard with a frowning expression. 'Plan H' or the small print in his contract hopefully didn't stipulate the penalty for an eight-goal thrashing as being the surgical removal of a similar number of digits (Saudi Arabia being an absolute monarchy with a legal system based on Islamic tradition, a country governed by far fewer families than the 200 or so who make up the French establishment). In Germany, an offer of 5 per cent off Adidas sportswear for every goal scored resulted in a legally enforceable discount of 40 per cent for consumers (which considering the profit margin on this kind of product, still left manufacturer and retailer making money from each sale).

Realpolitik is of course a German expression, meaning politics based on practicalities rather than ideals, and by the time of this game it had been re-established in the wake of '9/11'. Afghanistan had been invaded and made free for democracy and feminism. Instead of being regarded as a military dictator and political pariah, brave and dashing General Musharraf of Pakistan had been rebranded as a moderate Muslim moderniser and friend of the West, causing high dudgeon and intense irritation to the Hindu government of India (which for all its faults and internal contradictions is, like Israel, a flawed but functioning democracy). Israelis and Palestinians were still killing each other in the moral monkey's armpit that is the Middle East, but on the day of the Germany–Saudi game Britons living in India or Pakistan were advised to leave by the Foreign Office (due to the long-simmering dispute over the status of Kashmir, which looked likely to end in conventional war – or even in an exchange of nuclear weapons). In the British media, however, the most dangerous nuclear stand-off since Cuba in 1962 was relegated to third place in newsroom running orders (behind the World Cup and the Queen's Golden Jubilee).

Germany 1 England 5. Germany 8 Saudi Arabia 0. Pakistan 0 India 0. Let's hope so, because there are no home wins, away victories or even score draws in nuclear wars. Just ask the deformed football fans of Alpha Centauri, in between bouts of vomiting caused by unexpected English successes or terminal radiation poisoning.

5. The Real Juan Sebastian Veron Stands Up

Argentina 1 Nigeria 0
Ibaraki, Sunday, 2 June, 6.30 a.m., BBC

Travelling through to the Big G from Embra on the Saturday night, in order to watch the England game with family and friends, the Scottish summer's first meteorological confluence of bright sunshine and high humidity had me in danger of succumbing to a full-on migraine.[1] Being surrounded by drunken rugby fans boarding the train at Haymarket had me cursing my anti-social bad luck. However, I enjoyed their cheerful company and shared some good crack (conversational not cocaine, which nevertheless like cocaine knocked the migraine on the head and staved off aching loneliness for 50 minutes). World Cup results and tournament prospects served as social glue, restarting cross-aisle banter whenever it threatened to run out of steam. My best line, which got a laugh, was a joke about Mick McCarthy's mobile ring-tone being changed to play the theme tune from *Mission Impossible*.

As one female journalist attending the England–Sweden game as a virginal in-situ supporter of her country remarked in print, all the international fixtures up to and including the first England game had been hooligan and hatred free (unlike the enmities engendered at club level, where for example Argentinian and Italian fans had been *killed* during violence-permeated local derbies in season 2001–02). The lack of street fighting in Seoul and Tokyo was partly explicable in terms of banned individuals being prevented from entering the host nations (circulated lists of *named* undesirables running to over 1,000 in number) and also because the expensive Far East locations economically weeded out the socio-economic DE-ers whose idea of a good time is getting tanked up and having a rumble with opposing fans. In addition, the polite cultural atmosphere imposed a 'Behave yourself' mentality on would-be hooligans, since fisticuffs and verbal violence would have been as inappropriate as such behaviour in a pre-school kindergarten back home, with innocent little eyes widening in real horror at adults kicking seven bells out of each other.

For this World Cup many middle-class Argentinians were in the same leaky financial boat as ordinary Nigerians, struggling just to survive at home without any prospect of indulging in the luxury of foreign travel. Indeed, the barter system had resurfaced in the Argentinian economy, with citizens trading skills for food and clothing. Even if you had pesos in a bank, getting them out and converted into dollars as their worth depreciated daily was a very good trick if you could pull it off.

Argentina, with its resources and educated workforce, should be the Latin-American Germany, the economic powerhouse of a continent, but its social and political instability is matched by a boom-and-bust economy that has been mismanaged in macro-economic terms for almost a century. So like the majority of those supporting arch-rivals Brazil, most Argentinian *hinchas* had to settle for a seat in front of the TV.

Keeping their eyes open during a soporific first-half must have been tiring, but in the second period Nigeria's highly-praised 'Super Eagles' simply disappeared from view (at least as an attacking force, but not as a source of retinal overstimulation, turning out at the Kashima Stadium in an all lime-green fluorescent ensemble that I would have preferred to see in soothing black-and-white monochrome).

Argentina were creating chances and playing impressively, and from a Juan Veron corner Gabriel Batistuta headed in from a breathtakingly acute angle at the far post. Game over. Batistuta being substituted with Lazio's £35 million striker Hernan Crespo must have made English match-assessor David Platt swallow hard at such an embarrassment of riches amongst their strongest Group F opponents. Manchester United's big-money disappointment Veron ran the game from central midfield (whereas under the barking direction of Sir Alex Ferguson at Old Trafford he is cast in the role of supporting actor to leading man and matinee idol David Beckham).

Back in Buenos Aires, the city centre streets and statue-strewn squares filled with celebrants rather than protestors and they partied until dawn with blue-and-white striped flags, firecrackers, unlicensed guns, whistles, trombones, drums, megaphones and blaring car horns. Those still with white-collar jobs to go to probably staggered into the office knackered but happy.

NOTES

[1] I've almost lost count of foreign friends and acquaintances who have been studying or working in Scotland for a year but have almost packed their bags early because of the temperate but utterly dispiriting Scottish weather. Round about April/May they tend to hit a mental wall, as grey sunless skies continue into spring, and those visitors from south of the Alps or Australia have to psyche themselves up each morning to face going out into drizzling rain and/or cold winds. One suicidal Spanish student almost taxied straight to Edinburgh Airport when I told her that we don't get long, hot summers in Scotland (anymore), just year-long winters that eventually lose their shivering edge for a few months. An Australian co-worker sought solace in Leith Walk bars and when persuaded to wrap up warm for a game of tennis on the public courts in Holyrood Park couldn't believe they were closed until a semi-official opening in June (the council having withdrawn funding, leaving local volunteers trying to keep the courts and bowling greens open for business). 'No wonder you guys are crap at sport, mate' she mused morosely into her pint of Foster's. I lost the first set 7–6 on a tie-break when we eventually got on, but I retired hurt with a suspected heart attack trailing 4–1 in the second set. As a fast bowler who has played for her state, she didn't have to take her frustration at a sunless existence out on me, a mere good rabbit on public courts, with 'a sissy serve like a bloody dunny handle being pulled by a pox doctor's clerk'. Cheers, mate.

6. And for Those Watching in Black-and-white . . .

Paraguay 2 South Africa 2
Busan: Sunday, 25 June, 8.30 a.m., ITV and ITV2

Still bleary-eyed after getting up early for the previous 6.30 a.m. kick-off, I finally opened my mother's Venetian blinds. It was cold and wet outside – surprise, surprise – which explained my ice-cold bare feet (along with Reynaud's Disease). I switched on the gas fire and wondered how my septuagenarian mum ended up living in modern minimalist style (with an exposed hardwood floor and cool leather sofas) while I rented a room and kitchen with second-hand furniture. She worked hard all her days and has consummate good taste, I guess.

Paraguay is famous for its dictatorships, especially Alfredo Stroessner's, and although it has gone to war against America, Britain, Brazil, Argentina and Uruguay it normally only invades northern neighbour Bolivia 'to quell political instability' (in the form of over 400 Bolivian revolutions since independence in 1825). Its current president described South Africa as the worst team in the competition, much to the annoyance of the 'Bafana Bafana' (South Africa's name for their football team, not their current president).

Ex-President Nelson Mandela is the only politician in the world who I can honestly say I admire and respect without qualification. I'm embarrassed to admit that as an early 20-something I actually agreed with some publicity-seeking Tory councillor who objected to renaming a square in Glasgow after the great man (who was languishing in a Boer jail at the time). I also argued that just because I *preferred* being white to black that didn't make me racist (which it bloody well did actually, but my political consciousness has risen to the point where the very idea of being 'proud' to be white – not that I ever was, as such – makes me blush beetroot red, but if I had my way as the president of a world government I'd instigate a 500-year-plan to populate the world with coffee-coloured atheists of international-citizen status). A couple of years ago I saw Mandela at the bottom of Edinburgh's Lothian Road, leaving the Caledonian Hotel to get into his chauffeur-driven limousine. I shouted, 'Nelson! Keep up the good work!' and he smiled and waved back. It made my afternoon and my only regret is that I didn't sprint through the heavy traffic to get myself photographed with him, shaking hands and smiling for my £19.99 Miranda camera (which I had in my backpack). I'd have had multiple copies made up, with one blown up to life-size and professionally framed. Fuck – sometimes I just don't think *fast* enough . . .

Without eccentric keeper and free-kick taker Jose Luis Chilavert in goal for Paraguay, only a headed goal from Roque Santa Cruz enlivened a dull first half. The excitement and drama was saved for the second half, which ITV in their marketing wisdom chose to switch to ITV 2 Digital. The money-mad executive suits had decided that a studio-bound Des Lynam introducing 'the build up to the big game' between England and Sweden offered greater potential advertising revenues – even if the viewing audience on terrestrial was deprived of the great, or at least 'live', goals. Without cable, satellite or digital television, my mother had inadvertently deprived me of the chance to see 64 live games in their entirety. I don't subscribe to any of these services either, but if she'd had the foresight to warn me I could have phoned round neighbours and friends – or even taken a taxi into town and found a bar or shop window showing the second half *live*. Being a loving son and mature man, I of course bit my tongue when she finally got out of bed but I was literally swallowing blood in frustration, I can tell you. And apparently one million Germans without a box, cable or satellite missed their eight goals against the Saudis, because the Kirsch Corporation would not sell the live rights to the German equivalent of the BBC.

When the ITV programme schedulers finally deigned to transmit the second half to aerial-only Luddites, it was a highlights-only package. When Paraguay scored a scorching second, commentator Peter Drury remarked on the surprising physical joy displayed by a coach who was 'a septuagenarian'.

'Pardon?' responded match analyser David Pleat.

'A 70-year-old to you, David.'

'And in Korean?'

'I'll leave that to you, David!'

Jee-zuz! With this kind of dialogue, I'll be turning down the sound and listening to Radio Five Live instead, I thought. As a septuagenarian male and Roman Catholic, Cesare Maldini could be the next Paraguayan *presidente* – except he's Italian and, despite having coached the Italian squad in World Cups, with a degree of success, is a hugely unpopular figure in Paraguay.

One Estanislao Struway – whose name sounds like a Ferengi out of *Star Trek* – got Bafana Bafana back in the game with a spectacular own goal; then with a minute left to play South Africa got a penalty. Manchester United reserve Quinton Fortune stepped up to take it, but before starting his run-up Chiqui Arce passed wind and told him he'd miss it. He scored to make it 2–2 and although such mind games are very unsporting it would have been nice to see such incidents live as they happened. I mean, ITV had 15 bloody minutes to spare *after* this great game ended.

7. Sven Still Boogieing, Des?

By 10 a.m. everyone was up from their IKEA 'Lonelies', inflatable camping mattresses or flowery four-poster beds or down from their rafters, out of their trees or up from their lairs – and I was faced with the prospect of a full English breakfast. Normally I breakfast on a smorgasbord of coffee, milk, Sweetex, Nurofen Plus, Dif 118s, Lucozade and Marlboro Reds, a post-10 eating regime that has seen me lose two stones in weight and which if extended to cover lunch and dinner and written up as a self-help diet book would probably make me a bestselling writer (all be it one who became invisible when viewed sideways, like the autobiographical authors Posh Spice and Geri Halliwell, whose writing talent is about as thin as their horribly emaciated bodies, but who publish bloody fat books).

My replica England shirt was only a medium, which was good, but it was a Euro '96 version and therefore naffly out-of-date (but not old enough to be worn with pride as an example of retro-chic, like my priceless Dukla Prague away kit circa 1976). The World Cup 2002 strip for the English squad was made by Umbro and was one of the most aesthetically pleasing in decades, with a single red stripe down one side and set off with subtle blue piping. Kappa's kit for the Italians was great in catwalk theory, since its tightly tailored fit required an ironing-board flat stomach, such as possessed by Francesco Totti and Alessandro Del Piero, but which when worn by middle-aged Milanese builders with beer bellies was going to look hideously stretched.

Most of the other nations had their kit supplied by Adidas or Nike,[1] but it is maybe worth noting that for season 2002–03 both Celtic and Rangers have requested that their kit manufacturers try to

47

accommodate the demand amongst their fans for replica tops that come in sizes up to and including XXXL (although I'd have thought that if you were that fat your season ticket to Parkhead or Ibrox should be withheld on the grounds of safety, since such obesity in a football stand must constitute a fire hazard; not by increasing the risk of spontaneous combustion obviously – although I don't know about that for sure – but making evacuation in the event of a blaze more difficult to organise without bottlenecks developing).

With my charity-shop England top, a can of Boddingtons and a pack of Benson & Hedges I felt patriotic and working class, rather than politically right-wing and proletarian. With my 30 quid on at 9–1, I was already spending in my head the £300 that would be coming back to me after 30 June, thanks to the abolition of the 10 per cent betting levy that Tony Blair's 'socialist' government had apparently regarded as undesirable regressive taxation on the poor (or possibly unacceptable progressive taxation on the rich like Ladbroke's).[2]

I was, then, rooting for England for the sake of financial remuneration but was I really about to throw over 30-odd years of social conditioning to support them in my heart as well as my head? Maybe I was half way there, because I didn't give a damn about new Scotland boss Bertie Vögts having got off to a 0–4 start to his stewardship. Scotland are literally beyond a joke (unlike the Jamaican bob-sleigh team, say, who are genuinely funny).

I was fairly confident that England would get off to a winning start in the 'Group of Ceasing to Exist Forever'. After all, Captain Metatarsal (David Beckham) was back from injury and the Swedes had just lost their defensive linchpin and captain, Patrik Andersson of Barcelona, to a hamstring injury picked up in training. Liverpool's Emile Heskey in the role of left-winger, however, was surely a sleight-of-hand selection trick by Sven-Göran Eriksson to lull his opposition numbers – co-coaches Tommy Soderberg and Lars Lagerback (who sounded like a pair of IKEA bookcases) – into a false sense of sniggering security.

With only Beckham and Michael Owen capable of challenging for a place in a hypothetical World XI, was Eriksson capable of transforming footballing lead into soccer gold? Would he take a page out of the coaching manual of Charles XII of Sweden – an 18th-century monarch who created chaos while rampaging across Europe beating far larger and better-equipped armies? Cold, calm Charles was inspired by a biography of Alexander the Great, who he was determined to emulate in a European context. Peter the Great of Russia was sent packing while poor old Augustus the Strong of Saxony–Poland was harried all over his empire in a zig-zag of unstoppable away wins. Charles was planning to invade England with a fleet of ships leased from the pirates of Madagascar and would probably have succeeded if not for a stray rock knocking him dead in a minor battle during a little local difficulty in Sweden. Was Sven inspired by Alexanderism – nothing or everything! – or bloody bourgeois Bonapartism, with its calculated risk taking for on balance victories? Would Sven secretly be happy with second-round qualification and honourable defeat or was he certifiably confident enough to be expecting a crowning glory to his coaching career in Yokohama?

Eriksson looks and talks like a school principal from his small Swedish home town of Tronsby, but he has a coaching CV that starts with tiny Degerfors and via Gothenburg, Benfica, Roma, Fiorentina, Sampdoria and Lazio ends with the sleeping international giant of England. On the plus side, he won the Serie A scudetto with Lazio, but on the negative his nickname amongst critics in Italy was 'Perdente di Successo' ('The Successful Loser'), having lost Serie A titles from winning positions with both Lazio and Roma. His alleged affair with über-babe Ulrika Jonsson was in questionable taste if sexually consummated, and certainly poorly timed, adding nothing to his sexual-charisma rating, since blonde-bombshell TV presenters are two-a-kroner in dumbed-down Britain. It was hardly comparable with Marilyn Monroe and Albert Einstein (or even Arthur Miller). Or Ingrid Bergman and Roberto Rossellini. (Interestingly, the Swedes buy ten times as many books as Brits per head of the population, but Brits own twice as many videos per capita.) Now if Sven had been caught *in flagrante delicto* with Kylie Minogue, Kim Basinger or even Princess Stefanie of Monaco . . .

How would the Swedish team actually play, schizophrenically unpredictable as groups of Swedes tend to be? As a country they spend more on social welfare than anyone else, enjoy a high standard of living and excellent quality of life, yet top European league tables for abortion, divorce, suicide and murder. Emergency admissions to psychiatric hospitals are the third highest in the world (behind Wales and Venezuela). The football team is similarly manic when up and depressive when down.

Despite having no international, never mind world-class, defenders England took almost total control from kick-off. Soderberg looked suicidal on the touchline, Lagerback certifiable and Sven sexually satiated. England were doing nothing remarkable, simply passing short and moving for the return, while tackling like feral cats. The Swedes looked close to tears and were playing as if they had already been eliminated. A trademark Beckham corner was met by big Sol Campbell and England were ahead. And I was up and out of my mother's rocking chair, cheering and air punching.

Sven and the squad's head doctor had been featured on the BBC 2 science programme *Horizon* and supposedly some Swedish psychologist called Willi something had succeeded in identifying and eliminating aspects of a losing mentality. I was immediately suspicious, because the behaviourist approach being adopted seemed to have very little in common with the theoretical groundwork laid down by the geniuses Freud and Jung (*who weren't even mentioned!*). Under Kevin Keegan, half the England team looked as if they took to the field dreaming about having sex with their mothers and fantasising about killing their fathers (and if the bloody Germans subconsciously desire the opposite, they still have a World Cup record to die for). We didn't even learn if Beckham had been a bed-wetter or if Owen suffered from premature ejaculation.

In the second half, the Swedes were transformed from morose extras in an Ingmar Bergman movie into up-for-it Viking warriors. The psychological change was positively Adlerian (and just because Adler died poor and embittered in *Aberdeen* of all places, it doesn't lessen the validity of his theoretical insights). England were playing like guilty and fearful schoolboys caught in acts of self-abuse with empty Lucozade bottles by neurasthenic mothers and awaiting the return from work of furiously repressed fathers.

Danny Mills tried to chest the ball back to David Seaman in a crowded penalty area, realised he was making a potentially fatal mistake and in panic mode blindly cleared the ball anywhere. It fell to Everton's Niclas Alexandersson (*Oh, no!*) who dropped a left shoulder and hit a shot so hard down Seaman's metaphorical throat that the English keeper nearly choked on it – its trajectory being eminently stoppable but not its velocity. Nicknamed 'Safe Hands' by Arsenal colleagues, Seaman nevertheless kept England in the game (and the tournament) thereafter.

With seconds left another error left Celtic's Henrik Larsson clear in on goal. His first touch was nervously heavy, but he should still have scored (instead screwing his shot wide of the far post).

'Disappointing but not disastrous,' I concluded to the assembled company. 'Just as well for *us* that Larsson's not a world class finisher.'

'Yes he is,' countered my Celtic-supporting sister crossly.

'No, he's not. Just a very good player at club level. He's aware of his limitations and therefore prefers to remain a big pike in the small goldfish bowl of the Scottish Premier League, rather than risk swimming out of his depth in Serie A or the Primera Liga.'

'Rubbish. He's as good as, if not better than . . . Raúl!'

'Right, and Johan Mjalby is as good if not better than . . . Roberto Ayala, Frank Leboeuf more like.'

Our mother told us both to calm down, whereupon I offered to wash up the breakfast dishes but only instead of 'writing up my notes while they were still fresh in my mind'. My mother then said she'd do them herself, although my sister expressed the opinion that if I didn't do them, she would (in addition to having made the breakfast). My mother said I couldn't be expected to wash up – 'because I was working' – which for some reason had my kid sister scowling (although my smirking probably didn't help). She left a couple of greasy streaks – I know, because I checked – and failed to brew me a coffee or make up my rumpled bed, as I had requested. I can't remember exactly what Tolstoy said about happy families being similar and unhappy families totally unique in their own way, but I'm sure he was on the familial money (to which my sister would probably make some withering comment about my not having read even one book by Tolstoy, never mind *Anna Karenina*, and to which I could only respond with: 'Yes I have. Twice. The second time in original *Russian*. Na-na-na . . .').

A gloomy ITV panel agreed that things could have been worse and ex-England manager and current Newcastle coach Bobby Robson sought solace in the fact that 'England are still on the dance floor'.

Des Lynam's eyes twinkled as he raised a trademark eyebrow.

'Still boogieing, Bobby, still boogieing.'

NOTES

[1] All the Adidas kit designs were produced from the same basic design template: the classic styling of the 1970s. France, Germany and Spain, for example, all sported the three famous stripes on each arm, proper collars and an instantly recognisable Adidas triangle logo on each breast. Nike, however, got their basic styling concept hysterically overwrought, to the aesthetic detriment of Russia, Belgium, Portugal and sacrilegiously Brazil.

If a mathematical formula, the Nike 'look' would have been wiped from a blackboard by any self-respecting professor who believed in the simple beauty of numbers and equations. The sacramental simplicity of the yellow jerseys had been ruined by the slapdash application of green 'contrast vents'. It was a real shame because the Nike swoosh logo is a design classic. Puma won the worst-design award for Paraguay's multi-coloured monstrosity of a strip (*and* for the all gold or champagne-coloured change kit into the basement bargain).

[2] When putting my money on England, I almost spent £2 on the Ladbroke's accumulator for the World Cup. Punters filled in a pre-printed form with the first 20 fixtures listed and won £1,000 for correctly guessing the first five results (as in win, lose or draw), increasing in multiples of five to the theoretical jackpot of one million quid for predicting all the first 20 games correctly. Game One was of course France versus Senegal and goal-scorer and coupon-buster Papa Bouba Diop must have saved this high-street bookmaking chain an absolute fortune. At least 95 per cent of the forms with their accompanying £2 entry fees must have become null and void after the first full-time whistle. If you ever see a bookie jumping off a bridge, follow him – he must be jumping into a river of used fivers, tenners and twenties. At the time, I almost filled in a form with a draw predicted for France–Senegal and I came close to punting a fiver on Senegal to actually win the competition (but stopped since the stake would have had to come out of my £30 on England). Senegal were 250/1!

8. Hola Picasso, Adios Dali

Spain 3 Slovenia 1
Gwangju: Sunday, 2 June, 12.30 p.m., BBC

The prospect of Day Three's fourth game in a televised row was a case of my football-feasting eyes feeling bigger than my soccer-digesting brain could cope with. Not to mention my much-loved but mouthy family and friends.

'Where the hell is Slovenia anyway?' I wondered aloud. 'No, don't tell me . . . the rear end of the old pantomime Czech donkey.'

'Actually, it's the tiny Alpine bit at the top of the now-defunct Yugoslavia,' my sister's significant other informed us all. 'The smallest populated country to participate in the finals since Northern Ireland in Spain in . . . erm . . .'

'Eighty-six!'

'. . . Eighty-two, I think you'll find, David.'

'Northern Ireland's a province, not a country per se, technically speaking.'

'Don't be such a pedantic prima donna,' shouted my sister.

'Alright then: can either of you tell me how many countries there are in the world, if the UK counts as just one?'

'One-hundred and . . . ninety–' I thought her fella had finished saying.

'Wrong, mate, I'm sorry to say. Close but no cigar. It's actually one-hundred and–'

'. . . ninety-three, if you include the recently independent East Timor, which split from–'

'*Malasyia.* I know.'

'Indonesia, as a matter of strict fact, David. But you're close enough for a cigar I'd say.'

'What are you laughing at?'

'You, as a matter of strict fact – my know-it-all big brother, who just *occasionally* gets it wrong. "The pantomime rear-end of the old Czech donkey"! Honestly, if you don't know, just say so!'

'I did know, actually. I just got mixed up when I spoke because it's such a bloody competitive environment in here when it comes to stupid general knowledge questions . . . What's for lunch?'

'Sweet FA for you.'

'Mum, will you tell her to shut the hell up? I'm getting a migraine.'

'Be quiet, the pair of you!'

'He started it.'

'No I didn't.'

'Did too.'

'Did not.' ·

'For heaven's sake, it's hard to believe one of you is 33 and the other . . . eh . . .'

'For fuck's sake, Mum – *41.*'

'Watch your language in *my* home, David!'

'Well . . . How come you can remember how old *she* is but not me?'

'Because Mum loves me *more*, that's why!'

'No I don't! Of course I don't!'

'At least I was *planned*, not a family planning accident who *happened along* . . .'

'But a very happy one for your late father and me . . .'

'Give us the remote over here, you.'

'Get lost, *big bro.*'

'Mum! I need it for *researching* what's on the other channels for my book.'

'Give it to your brother.'

'Tssh . . . Here, *catch.*'

'Hoi! Did you see that, Mum? She could have put me eye out.'

'Sometimes I wish I had a blindfold and ear-plugs when you two start arguing . . . I suppose there's no chance of any grandchildren in the foreseeable future?'

In filial unison and smiling broadly at each other: 'For God's sake, Mum! We're still young!'

Raúl Gonzalez, or 'Raúl', put Spain ahead but I'm not sure that the

Real Madrid superstar has really earned the shorthand diminutive by which he is universally known (unlike the genuinely great Pelé – or Edson Arantes do Nascimento as he was christened). Pelé looked and played like a supremely athletic artist, whereas Raúl looks off-the-street unprepossessing – and a little bit silly in his distinctive white boots (which clash stridently with the royal-blue Spanish socks). Still, his buy-out clause at Real stipulates £117 million to secure his services elsewhere and he is married to beautiful model 'Mamen'. Nevertheless, even on the cover of glossy lifestyle magazines like *Hola!* he bears an uncanny facial resemblance to Steve Coogan's comic creation Alan Partridge.

Zlatko Zahovic, Slovenia's 'Zlatko', was substituted by coach Srecko Katanec (who at 38 was the youngest ever coach at a World Cup). Zealous Zlatko was understandably apoplectic and like Roy Keane promptly packed his bags, or matching set of Vuitton suitcases, for his early return to Benfica and Portugal. The Slovenian Football Association apparatchiks intervened, or refused to return Zlatko's passport, and he was forced to try and make it up with coach Srecko (which he reportedly did from six paces away with his Gucci handbag, so to speak) – and the Irish thought they had problems with 'creative differences'. Despite equalising, Slovenia were comfortably beaten 3–1.

Spain hadn't won an opening fixture in a World Cup since 1952 – such notoriously slow starts usually resulting in the Spanish sleeping giants being sent home early – and their national team's record of chronic underachievement was a genuine mystery when compared with the country's club record of success at European level, achieved by the likes of Valencia, Barcelona and of course Real (who triumphed again in the Champions League final of 2002 at Hampden Park, thanks, it should be noted, to the scoring heroics of *Frenchman* Zinedine Zidane). The number of foreign stars playing in Spain is often used as an excuse or explanation, but the Serie A league has always run a bigger balance-of-payments deficit when it comes to importing foreign players and Italy's national record is exemplary. But the Spanish had at last kicked off as if being painted for posterity by Picasso instead of being surrealistically written off by the likes of Salvador Dali (whose nickname of 'Avida Dollars', Zlatko could probably relate to).

In intense heat and high humidity, Spain coach Jose Camacho looked smart and stylish in collar and tie, but overweight and uncomfortable with massive damp patches showing under his armpits. Footage of Camacho may well be recycled by the makers of Lynx male deodorant, who were one of ITV's main advertisers for the duration of the tournament, with a tagline about the product lasting for at least 24 hours.[1] Which is longer than the great Zlatko lasted in the World Cup . . .

NOTES

[1] The Lynx ads, being produced for the New Lads' market, are quite sexy but the most arousing commercial I have ever seen was running on ITV during this World Cup. It features a stunning blonde in a mini-type ra-ra skirt walking two cute dogs. An equally attractive pair of female passers-by stop her and ask if they can stroke 'them'. Whereupon a camera positioned in the gutter shoots four female hands running up and down her smooth legs (and if the camera had been shooting from a slightly more acute angle male viewers would have been able to tell whether the actress had actually 'gone commando' for the scene or not). This commercial's 'sexiness' actually prompted physical symptoms of arousal for this viewer, but as an ad designed to shift a product it sadly has to be classified a complete failure, since I cannot remember the brand name or even the generic product being flogged. Nivea? Skin moisturiser? I know Scholl the sandal people are currently advertising a lotion for *feet*, but as the author of *The Denial of Death*, E. Becker pointed out: 'Nothing equals the foot for ugliness.' Bare human feet are almost invariably *disgusting*, with the exception of a few pretty girls' and my own, and I don't want to go there in TV commercials, thank you very much, unless concentrating on nylons and stilettoes . . .

9. Blanco, Blanco, the Mexican Kangaroo

Croatia 0 Mexico 1
Niigata: Monday, 3 June, 7.30 a.m., BBC

If the Falkland's War between Britain and Argentina was memorably described as resembling 'two bald men fighting over a comb', this opening Group G fixture could be summarised as two impotent lounge lizards arguing over a condom. Croatia of course was once part of a united socialist federation called Yugoslavia, held together by the personality cult promulgated by President Josip Tito, but after the fall of communism it was never going to hold together – consisting as it did of Serbia, Croatia, Slovenia, Bosnia-Herzegovina, Macedonia and Montenegro. I admit I had to look up the full list of these combatants and neutral bystanders in the wars of 'ethnic cleansing' which followed, and upon reflection I'm less inclined to be sarcastic about Americans who can't fit Northern Ireland, Wales, Scotland and England together properly in the UK jigsaw because of their insular and isolationist frames of geographical reference. Unlike the Christian Eastern Orthodoxy which prevailed in Serbia, Croatia chose to follow the course of Roman Catholicism (back when the Church of Rome split in two). Mexico, too, is a stronghold of the latter faith, but according to my reference books is quite amazingly *eight* times the size of Britain (but with a similar population). (Being a big fan of *The West Wing* I was surprised to learn while watching a recent episode on Channel 4 that the traditional map of the world, with Europe in the centre and located in the 'northern hemisphere', is totally out of physical proportion – with Greenland being overestimated in size compared to Africa for example.)

Both teams in Niigata were ageing fast and put on performances worthy of crotchety old-age pensioners. The only highlight was a second-half penalty, which saw Cuauhtemoc Blanco being hacked down by Boris Zivkovic. Co-commentator Trevor Brooking asked Barry Davies, 'Is that the longest run-up you've ever seen?', Blanco requiring about 30 yards in distance to prepare for the resulting conversion.[1] He failed to pull off another kangaroo hop, however, with the ball between his ankles and two closing-in defenders (as successfully performed to great applause in France '98). This time he landed on his well-padded backside.

The only other incident of note was Mirko Jozic's bizarre managerial decision to replace *solo* striker Alan Boksic with substitute Mario Stanic of Chelsea (who is an out-and-out *midfielder*). As a peroxide blond Stanic stood out as a target man; as a lone centre-forward with the clock ticking down to defeat he just looked out of place, annoyed and angry. In France '98, Croatia finished a commendable third, but on the evidence of this game they looked as if they would be hard pushed to finish third above Ecuador in Group G.

NOTES

[1] I half-expected Blanco to enliven his long run-up with a hop, step and jump, *à la* Jonathan Edwards (the British hop-step-and-jump Olympic Champion), but disappointingly he failed to do anything out of the ordinary. Whether Welsh, English, Scottish or Northern Irish, I think we can all be proud of born-again Christian Jonathan, because this is a blue-ribbon event with intense worldwide competition for the most coveted gold medal in athletics – unlike the truly silly long-jump (which was probably invented to cater for those mediocre athletes who couldn't cope with the technical difficulties involved in hop, step and jumping). Bet you can't name the current holder of the long-jump gold medal. Bob Beaman in the Mexico City Olympics did achieve a remarkable distance, I grant you, but this longstanding world-record for the long-jump just shows that the event normally only attracts the second rate.

10. Turkey for Breakfast, Lunch and Dinner

Brazil 2 Turkey 1
Ulsan: Monday, 3 June, 10 a.m., BBC

Before this match, Brazil as a footballing world superpower were supposedly 'ancient history' – like the Soviet Union and any alternative to capitalism – and by only *just* qualifying for this World Cup they nearly experienced their own Berlin Wall collapsing on top of them. After a fairly honourable defeat to France in the '98 final, Brazil went on to record losses against the likes of Ecuador, Honduras and Bolivia (with the corporate circus of 'Team Nike' chalking up goodwill defeats against South Korea and Australia). The medical notes on Ronaldo's knee could have been turned into scripts for a popular daytime soap-opera in Rio de Janeiro.

If the decline of Brazil had been limited to poor results, it would have been bearable to the many football purists who admire them, but the attacking-and-entertaining philosophy had been discarded by a succession of desperate coaches (and even Luiz Felipe Scolari, who had succeeded in cajoling his nervous charges over the qualifying line, was a cynical proponent of muscle and organisation rather than a true believer in brains and rhythm). But Brazil *are* different, whether you're talking about the country or the team.

The country is unique in Latin America in that its official tongue is Portuguese, courtesy of Christopher Columbus, whose appalling-to-non-existent navigational skills should have resulted in Queen Isabella of Spain forbidding him to take charge of anything bigger than a Madrid rowing boat. The 'discoverer' of America (*pace* Leif Ericson) in the form of islands in the Bahamas and Cuba (on which he confidently expected to be received by the Grand Khan of China) managed to claim El Salvador for the Spanish crown but somehow contrived to overlook the slightly larger and more important land mass of Brazil. Because of its staggering geographical dimensions, the Portuguese imported 15 million African slaves to work the rich land (but didn't kill nearly as many indigenous peoples as the gold-obsessed Spaniards). Brazil's football team is loved by fans around the globe, for many of whom Brazil are a natural second team after their own national sides. Whether winning, or occasionally losing, the Brazilians play with creative joy – what writing critics refer to as *jouissance* when it appears on the page in works of literature. They play to win, certainly, but also to enjoy themselves and entertain others. Any team that could parade the combined talents of Pelé and Garrincha had to have something special about it (the former a public relations dream for the Beautiful Game, the latter a tragic hero whose life off the pitch amounted to a series of sad own goals).

Turkey as a Muslim empire once controlled a third of Europe and all of the Middle East (under the Ottamans).[1] Mustafa Kemal, or Atatürk, dragged Turkey kicking and screaming into the 20th century (in 1922) and today it is a modern, moderate Muslim state (albeit a slightly schizophrenic one, with less than 5 per cent of its land mass being technically 'in Europe', the rest being defined as 'Asian'). Although a member of NATO (along with, any day now, Russia), Turkey is keen to join that most Eurocentric of organisations, the European Union, but if Greece has a veto against new members they'll probably have a long wait. The national team have been improving steadily for years, and Galatasary actually won the UEFA cup with a majority of home-grown players in the team that overcame Leeds United and Arsenal on the way to the final. As a country they won't have to wait another 48 years before their next appearance on the World Cup stage.

An understudy was required for midfield hard man and inspirational captain Emerson, who 'Big Phil' Scolari had put in goal during a training session and who had dislocated a shoulder making a diving save. Big Phil must have been cursing such bad luck, which had been caught on TV cameras, but because football is *not* rocket science, an enforced change in the chemical make-up of the fuel can sometimes create an explosive mixture that takes off on the pitch like a bat out of hell. 3–5–2 became 4–4–2, with no Emerson in the middle digging trenches across the grass and waving his fist as he implored Brazil to go over the top one more time. Instead the Brazilian cavalry charge was lead by Ronaldo, looking match fit and mentally confident for the first time in four years, and orchestrated from midfield by Rivaldo, like Alexander taming a wildly rearing Bucephalus. Rustu Recber of Fenerbache looked like an extra from *The Pirates of Penzance* but he performed enough heroics in goal to inspire his outfield players – and with half-time approaching Turkey had recovered their second wind. Yildaray Basturk released a reverse pass that was positively Brazilian in conception and execution and Hasen Sas lashed it past Marcos (and it was strange to see a Brazilian team without – shall we say – statuesque Tafarel between the posts).

Nil–one. Game on. With additional knobs. Big Phil being 'philosophical' during the team talk, maybe even languidly lighting a cigar with a hundred-dollar bill (I don't think).

Five minutes after the restart, and following a lung-bursting run, Ronaldo stretched out a leg that must be insured for more than one of Betty Grable's in modern-day monies to secure a deserved equaliser. The Samba beat was building to a crescendo and the Turks were sweating like prisoners in *Midnight Express*. A criminally miss-hit goal-kick from Rustu resulted in Luizao bearing down on the perpetrator, and Alpay of Aston Villa committed the expected professional foul. Despite being well outside the penalty box a penalty was awarded and last-man Alpay sent packing by homer referee Kim Young-Joo. With only five minutes remaining, the Turks went loco in the Acapulco of South Korea (the holiday resort of Ulsan). Rivaldo, not surprisingly, scored. The Turks then started falling out of their trees like mad monkeys turning on a cruel scientist. The far-side linesman was trying to 'blank' the appeals from the increasingly tonto Turks and the camera zoomed in to capture his impression of impassiveness. Commentator Steve Wilson and analyser Joe Royle snickered at his obvious discomfort and he was a weird-looking character, a balding Eurasian with bug-out eyes and downcurled lower lip. The Mansu Stadium video director put up a giant reaction shot of his features and the linesman looked on the verge of a nervous breakdown.

In injury time, Rivaldo was wasting time at the far corner flag and Hakan Unsal kicked the ball at him, which ricocheted harmlessly off the skinny Brazilian's hip. Rivaldo clutched his *head* and collapsed dramatically (a performance that cost him a $10,000 fine). Unsal was sent off, where he *reluctantly* went. The linesman had only been a few feet away, but instead of helping his referee he continued to stare straight ahead, as if afraid that all the attention that he was inadvertently drawing to himself was in danger of exposing him to the watching world as an alien in bodysnatching human form. Of course, that was the explanation! His lizard-like alien tongue had snapped out for a nano-second and stung poor old Rivaldo in the eyes with its extraterrestrial venom. And he was praying telepathically for his mother ship overhead to beam him up before the Turks ripped his skin away to reveal reptile scales all over his body (whereupon the South Korean fans would have him for dinner). Either that or he was a doppelgänger for Desmond Morris of *Naked Ape* fame.

Young-Joo blew the full-time whistle almost immediately 90 minutes were up, his hopes of officiating at the World Cup final shattered. 'We took control of the game,' argued Turkish coach Senol Gunes, 'but we could not control the referee.'

Ooo, controversial or what?

Thankfully Sunderland boss Peter Reid wasn't still on the panel back in Auntie Beeb's studio. Like Gazza, he isn't the most articulate or interesting of ex-players but he didn't appear to be doing any homework whatsoever on the teams he was being paid to comment upon, not even recognising Blanco in the day's earlier game. Presenter Ray Stubbs had reacted to crowd shots of attractive young Brazilian women in braless T-shirts by observing: 'They're great up front those Brazilians,' to which likeable but limited Reid had chortled back: 'Steady on, lads!'. What the hell was the frequency for Radio Five Live, I wondered once more. At least Reid didn't shout, 'Get yer tits out, girls!'

Gary Lineker was in charge of panellists Alan Hansen, Martin O'Neill and Mark Lawrenson for the post-match Brazil–Turkey analysis, all of whom could talk for their respective countries without deviation, repetition or hesitation. In Hollywood terms, Lineker was coming across well, like Billy Crystal presenting the Oscars, with Hansen as a passable Cary Grant, O'Neill an entertaining Groucho Marx and Lawrenson a hangdog Jimmy Stewart or Bela Lugosi.

NOTES

[1] The date of the fall of Constantinople is burned into my memory – *1453!* – because as a teenager revising for O Grades, I became so obsessed with finding out the date of its fall to the non-Christian hordes that my father had to drive to the Mitchell Reference Library to look it up. He became a bit concerned about my mental state when he realised that I wasn't even sitting history as a subject at any point, but it had become so important to me that I was clambering around in the loft looking for an old encyclopaedia the day before an exam in economics. I worked in the information somehow, in an essay answer about Malthus and population levels, and got an A. I just had a *compulsion* to find out, because I had once known the date and couldn't cope with the *frustration* at having *forgotten*, which at the stressed-out time seemed literally *unforgivable* and *inexcusable*. One day, information overload and data-retrieval problems will cause my mind to crash like a computer – but not before watching and writing up Game 64, thank you very much, Herr Head Doctor, which would be *unforgivable* and *inexcusable*. What do you mean, who won the World Cup in 1954? I don't know: Hungary? Uruguay? Brazil? Of course, *West Germany!* I must remember that now: West Germany in 1954 . . . How fast is the speed of light? Wait, I know this. *120,000-something miles per hour.* AAARRGGHHH!!! And what was the *name* and *nationality* of the assistant referee I have just been writing about? I didn't write it down because I was sure I'd remember! Talk about *unforgivable* and *inexcusable*. Maybe neat Lithium would help me think properly and clearly . . .

11. The Odyssey of Ulises de la Cruz

Italy 2 Ecuador 0
Sapporo: Monday, 3 June, 12.30 p.m., ITV

From the capital of Ecuador, Quito, 3,000 feet above sea level, via Hibernian's Easter Road ground in the shadow of Arthur's Seat, to Hokkaido Island's Sapporo where the 1972 Winter Olympics were held, the far-travelled 28-year-old wing-back for the 'Condors', Ulises de la Cruz, had clocked up even more mileage than semi-mythical Ulysses besieging Troy and having other exciting adventures across the Ancient World. Could he and his team-mates hold out as World Cup virgins for 90 minutes, never mind 10 years, against the free-scoring Azzuri of Italy (who had assembled a squad of such physical perfection and footballing talent that a modern-day Homer would have been required to do justice to their expected heroic exploits)?

Ecuador managed to keep a clean sheet for all of seven minutes, when £33 million Christian Vieiri fired in the opener. He soon added another, but Ecuadorian coach Hernan Gomez is not a man to panic while under fire, as he proved during the qualifying campaign when he was pistol-whipped and shot at (allegedly for not selecting the off-spring of an ex-president).

Italian coach Giovanni Trapattoni, who has collected more silverware at club level than your average Latin American dictator has pinned to his chest when waving at crowds from presidential balconies, seemed satisfied and the Azzuri began to run the clock down.

Teenage Japanese girls in the stadium and watching on TV must have sighed in disappointment when the delightfully handsome Francesco Totti was subbed, but squeals of delight surely welcomed his replacement – the even more gorgeous Alessandro del Piero. If these two pin-ups are still unmarried or unpartnered, their sex lives must be like something out of *The Kamasutra* rewritten by the Marquis de Sade and Casanova. If you're a beautiful Japanese secretary, sitting in a Tokyo nightclub with your attractive best friend, who would you flutter your eyelids at: Totti and Del Piero at the zinc bar counting their millions or BBC commentators Barry Davies and John Motson, filling out their expenses at the next table?

'Ah so, Bally, Gooru! You have scored, yes? This sheepskin coat lookie good on my bedroom flooro . . .'

Who knows what life has in store for Ulises de la Cruz? Gennaro Gattuso came on as a sub for the Azzuri and unless I am very much mistaken, this is the same Rene Gattuso that Glasgow Rangers moved on a few years back because he was not deemed to be of sufficient quality for the Scottish Premier League. Australian-born Vieiri could have been a first-class cricketer for New South Wales instead of a striker for Inter Milan, or have found himself propping up the bar in a one-horse town in the outback, muttering in Oz-accented Italian about how he could have been a contender with the Italian club giants, rather than ending up in 'the back of beyond, mate, where the crows fly backwards to keep the dust out of their eyes'. So be polite to your Hibernian colleagues, Ulises, even if they don't seem as attractive as Circe, Scylla, Charybdis or other lotus-eaters; and beware of the Sirens, in the form of agents, directors or journalists, lest they lead you astray. There are worse places in the world to find yourself than Edinburgh's Easter Road (although it may be hard to believe on a freezing January afternoon, with easterly gales from the North Sea buffeting the stands and Motherwell players trying to kick lumps out of you).

The Scottish connections with this World Cup were depressingly limited. Apart from Ulises at Hibs, the only Scottish clubs to provide playing participants were Celtic, Rangers and Aberdeen (in the form of Henrik Larsson and Johan Mjalby with Sweden; Peter Lovenkrands and Jesper Christianson with Denmark; and Peter Kjaer, also with Denmark – and the last two are both *reserve* goalkeepers with their respective clubs and country).

Since Monday was a Bank Holiday in the UK, we got a half-decent film on BBC 2 in the afternoon: *The Great Gatsby*. I was still enjoying the novelty of seeing non-monochrome movies in colour on my (mother's) Akura, but Francis Ford Coppola's 1974 attempt to film F. Scott Fitzgerald's great American novel can only be described as an interesting failure. Its production values were almost as lavish as those thrown at the Golden Jubilee celebrations and I caught a nauseating glimpse of Jamie Theakston, the celebrity presenter, interviewing the impresario who was organising that evening's party and concert at Buckingham Palace to celebrate Queen Elizabeth II's 50 years on the throne – namely alternative comedian Ben Elton. In my opinion he's neither radical nor funny. But it'll soon be 'Sir Ben Elton' I've no doubt. Elton and his ilk remind me of the 'Octobrists' in Russia in 1905, negotiating compromise with Tsar Nicholas II (or 'Tsar Nick' as forelock-tugging but cutely informal Sir Ben would no doubt have called him). I'm well aware that the 1917 Revolution went right off the human-rights rails, but the royal Romanovs did have to be removed, completely, from the overall political picture. Come the next revolution, I'm looking forward to storming Buckingham Palace and personally banning the popular novels of Mr Elton (on the grounds of literary worthlessness rather than ideological unsoundness). And if he's ever nominated for the Booker Prize I'm going to self-immolate on the steps of the Guild Hall in protest.

NOTES

[1] Soon after the World Cup Ulises de la Cruz was transferred from Hibernian to Aston Villa in the English Premiership, for a remarkably generous transfer fee of £2 million.

12. Odds Against a Chinaman Playing for Dundee?

China 0 Costa Rica 2
Gwangju: Tuesday, 4 June, 7.30 a.m., BBC

'Sorry, mate, did I wake you up?'

'Nah . . . Just fell asleep watching that China–Costa Rica crap – the only advantage of doing back-shifts for the whole of June.'

'Look, is one of the Chinese team a registered player with Dundee FC?'

'Aye, the big centre-half.'

'Which one? And don't say they all look the same to you!'

'What's-'is-name? Fanny Wang?'

'Fan Zhiyi?'

'They all sound the same to me, Davie . . . But yeah, Dundee signed him at the start of the season thinking they'd sell millions of dark-blue replica shirts. Plus rake in exclusive Chinese TV rights to Dundee games.'

'Sounds reasonable. China's only other foreign-based player is Sun Jihai – with Manchester City.'

'Don't think they made anything but. Half the time he was unavailable because of qualifying games and Dundee probably had to foot the bill for the air fares back and forward. You know what Dundee are like – thought they'd make a fortune installing a dog-track for greyhound racing round Dens Park and lost a packet.'

'Right. Gotta go. Japan versus Belgium coming on ITV.'

'Are you coming back to the supermarket when you've finished the book?'

'No way. I'd rather starve and sleep on the streets. See ya later.'

A Chinaman playing at Dens Park for Dundee FC, Zhiyi must have experienced sociological displacement similar to his parents living through the Cultural Revolution of 1966–69. Any Costa Ricans lurking around the nether regions of the Scottish leagues, I wondered, thinking about the un-Spanish-sounding Harold Wallace and Steven Bryce? No Scots in the Chinese Premier Division, I'd bet (unless Scott Booth has ended up there after his spells with Aberdeen and at least one Bundesliga outfit).

China did not have a single 'Chang' in their team line-up or squad list, but Costa Rica had one William Sunsing listed as a substitute. The free movement of labour, if not capital, is I suppose a good thing but it's pretty confusing when names begin to lose their function as cultural baggage labels.

The China coach was, of course, called Bora Milutinovic, a footballing Red Adair who instead of being an on-call firefighter is a hired gunslinger for various national football associations. In the past this globetrotting Serb has taken over the reins for Mexico, Costa Rica, Nigeria and the USA in World Cups and led them *all* into the sunset of participation in the second round. Where are you, Bora, when Scotland needs you? Alexandre Guimaraes had played under Milutinovic when Costa Rica defeated Scotland in Italia '90, thanks to a goal by one Juan Cayasso (who today is hopefully serving time in the San Lucas penal colony), and, as the hip new young gunslinger in town, had guided Costa Rica to qualification ahead of both Mexico and America. So, Milutinovic was cast in the role of Master Khan and Guimaraes in the position of Kwai Chang Caine, or 'Grasshopper' from the TV classic from the 1970s *Kung Fu* (a chop suey Western). Italia '90 represented Grasshopper's training as a priest in China and South Korea–Japan 2002 the Wild East where pupil would confront master – and kick all the 'Confucius-he-say . . .' shit out of the old boy.

One coach had a population base of over a billion to draw on, the other just over a million and therefore there was only ever going to be one winner – and it wasn't going to be China!

China lost Manchester City's Jihai when he was carried off in agony, and with my *Kung Fu* consciousness kicking in I noticed that all four stretcher bearers were called 'LOC', obviously a family-run business in South Korean Gwangju. Then I realised that in other venues and in Japan the stretcher bearers had all been called 'LOC'. Could it be a Triad franchise, with the pseudo-injured players in most cases being garrotted in an attempt by FIFA to cut down on play-acting? With the Manchester City player removed, I was fast losing karmic serenity when Barry Davies kept referring to the Maine Road representative on the pitch – not another Chinaman but Costa Rica's Paulo Wanchope. Ricans Gil Martinez and Winston Parks played for, respectively, Brescia and Udineses in Serie A. This really was putting Scotland's defunct export trade in pro footballers to shame. Come back, Scott Booth, your crappy wee country needs you!

Nil–nil at half-time but Ronald Gomez eventually scored the goal Costa Rica deserved. Soon afterwards Mauricio Wright headed a second and whipped off his shirt to celebrate, only to be confronted by a misspelling of his family name in big white letters on the back of his bright red jersey: 'Wrigth'. Computers can get things wrong but to really screw up you need a human being. Speaking of which, commentator Davies had described the Chinese formation as being 'a sort of 4–3–1–1 system', which even if practised with high-flying kung-fu kicks probably couldn't be expected to overcome the handicap of playing with a man less than the opposition. Perennial BBC rival for the honour of 'getting' the final John Motson must have been struggling to maintain his meditative composure. In defence of Bazza and Motty I would say that at the very least they sound like themselves and nobody else, unlike the new breed of commentators who all sound very much alike and to my ears tend to morph indistinguishably into one another. With no Scotland on show, I missed Archie McPherson being behind the mike, since he comes across like Ron Atkinson with a massively expanded vocabulary and an encyclopaedic range of cultural references (which merge and metamorphose in Gertrude Stein-ish streams-of-consciousness commentaries that PhD alien students on Alpha Centauri are still trying to make literal sense of). For example: 'Facing a Ronald Koeman free-kick is like facing a serial killer.'

'Ah so. Grasshopper. I will leave you with two statements of fact to meditate upon: the Great Wall of China is the only man-made object visible from the moon; the flying saucers which crash-landed in Roswell, Arizona, were manned by little *yellow* men . . .'

'Master Po, Master Khan says you're a fat, blind bullshit artist!'

'Whatever. Here, go and stick a monkey on Costa Rica at 250/1 . . .'

13. A Fast Draw for Happy Hosts

Japan 2 Belgium 2
Saitama: Tuesday, 4 June, 10 a.m., ITV

As part of the festivities for the host nation's opening game, four military jets roared overhead in an unannounced fly-past (which prompted Clive Tyldsley to comment, 'At least, I hope that's what it is . . .'). Rumour had it that ground-to-air missiles had been deployed at all 20 World Cup venues, including Yokohama, which boasts Japan's tallest skyscraper, the Landmark Tower. For the first few minutes, the home players looked more nervous than energetic.

Belgian goalkeeper Geert de Vlieger had been complaining about the Fevernova match ball,[1] which makers Adidas assured the watching world was 'the roundest ever in World Cup history' (as compared to what, the oval spheres of France '98?). The Fevernovas were champagne-coloured with three red flamed logo segments. As well as travelling through space '10 per cent faster' (than what – bricks?), they had the unforeseen side-effect of making Belgian goalkeepers feel 'dizzy' (apparently).

Naming five famous Belgians is notoriously tough, but their footie teams normally provide at least a handful of funny handles and this squad was no exception: Danny Boffin, Bart Goor, Timmy Simons, Gaeten Englebert, Branco Struper and Wesley Sohk. Belgium is arguably the weirdest country in Europe judging by the recent revelations in the media about the prevalence of child molesters in Belgian society (making the statue of the small boy urinating in a Brussel's square – '*Mannekin Pis*' – the national symbol for a new millennium).

Japan is the most culturally difficult country for an outsider to try and comprehend. The Japanese, of either sex, are the least likely to marry a foreigner. Hierarchical organisation, a deference to authority and an obsession with not deviating from social etiquette are features of Japanese society that Westerners find difficult to take seriously. One character trait that beer-guzzling Belgians could relate to was the drinking-to-oblivion night life.

The Japanese do not commit suicide any more frequently than the Swedes and when they do it is called *jisatsu* not *hara kiri* (which is a belly-cutting rite derived from the Samurai codes of honour, and which requires a very, very good friend to decapitate the corpse – although suicidal Russian drunks with chainsaws have been known to perform this operation on themselves). No Belgian novelist ever plunged a sword into his stomach to show his contempt for critics and readers, unlike Yukio Mishima who disembowelled himself in full public view in 1970. Mishima was also 'un-Belgian' in that he was a body fascist who couldn't bear the thought of his muscular frame being doomed to decay (whereas Belgians are predisposed genetically to having Fevernova body shapes, their neighbours remarking of inedible food, 'Give it to the Belgians!').

The modern Japanese probably do share a little of their psyche with the Ancient Romans – via the Samurai connection – in that public failure of any significant kind can result in intense shame and the feeling that normal, honourable life is over (whereas in the West, the first reaction is to cover up wrongdoing, followed by blaming it on someone else and then as a last resort a spin-doctored attempt at restitution and redemption).[2]

Although the public in both Japan and South Korea seemed to have developed an over-inflated sense of their footballing prospects, the Japanese exhibited polite pride in their role of hosts, whereas the South Koreans displayed real passion about the whole event. Empty spaces in the stands were down to a ticketing fiasco, whereby unreturned briefs from, say, Argentina resulted in seats not being utilised. The professional J-League in Japan is less than ten years old, but the Saitama Stadium was a sell-out for the Belgian game.

In the last six World Cups Belgium have been like a Scotland side – but without access to a self-destruct button – getting off the ground successfully but never hitting truly great heights (although they did reach a semi-final in 1986). In the first half, the canny Belgians let the kamikaze Japanese blow themselves out and even took the lead after the restart; but by then the home team were flowing forward on a divine wind. Parma's Hidetoshi Nakata in midfield doesn't see eye to eye with French coach Phillippe Troussier and who knows if he was happy with his director in the big-budget Nike commercial (what with having to share airtime and close-ups with 15 other major superstars, which probably irritated him as much as Steve McQueen in *The Great Escape*), but he played as if being directed by Akira Kurosawa. Enough team-mates played to their maximum potential to merit casting in *The Seven Samurai*, whereas goal-scorer Marc '1,000 Volts' Wilmots wouldn't have had any co-stars if the rest of the Belgian team had been auditioning for a remake of *The Magnificent Seven*.

Like McQueen on his motorbike outrunning hundreds of Nazis with rubber bullets, Taka Suzuki drove through the Belgian midfield and defence to score (but managed to avoid getting heroically entangled in the goalframe netting/barbed wire). Junichi Inamoto, Arsenal's four-million-pound forgotten man with a mere four first-team appearances, hit a left-foot *ka–boomer* and Japan were ahead. Pudgy peroxide blond, he would finish the game as Man of the Match. The chagrined Belgians got their fat arses and old legs in gear and motored up the pitch for an equaliser, greeted by polite silence from 50,000 spectators. But they were soon screaming, shouting and chanting as Japan discovered what football can provide to fans when everything clicks together. Inamoto scored a dramatically satisfying winner, but the Costa Rican referee broke over a hundred million hearts by chalking it off for a mysterious infringement (probably because a flat-footed Belgian defender had cynically fallen over in Inamoto's unstoppable wake).

It ended 2–2 with four good goals and football played at 100 mph, constituting a 'fast draw' in J-League terminology. This was entertainment of the highest order, except for Belgian keeper De Vliegler and his outfield players, who all trooped off looking completely *dizzy*.

NOTES

[1] The regulation size of a football is based on the size of a man's head, because this was the first ever 'football' – reputedly that of a Danish warrior who the

Saxons decapitated. While waiting for the main battle against the Vikings to begin, they formed two sides and began kicking it around with swords for goalposts.

2 *The Savage God* by Al Alvarez is one of my all-time favourite books and I'd provide the sub-title if I could find the damn thing. If I've lent this to someone and they've topped themselves I'll never forgive myself, because it may well be out of print. It's a social history of suicide rather than a do-it-yourself manual and the only let down is the final section where the author switches from general overview to autobiographical self-dramatisation, describing his own attempt to kill himself. It's very well written, impressively researched and surprisingly amusing.

Ex-suicides, as compared to non-suicides, have a certain glamour attached to them, but by definition are a living contradiction in terms (and divide into the genuine and the phoney, the latter being in the majority but who tend to argue the sincerity of their self-destructive intention with the heated passion of the genuinely phoney). A real ex-suicide is definitely a cool thing to be, but to become one a non-suicide has to move beyond pseudo-suicide to such a degree that one has to run the real risk of breaking one's neck, choking on one's own vomit or bleeding to death in front of one's horror-struck eyes. Maybe the majority of suicides are in fact pseudo-suicides pushing their bad luck just a little too far. Certainly, the majority of ex-suicides are in fact self-dramatising non-suicides. Russian roulette for example has to be played using at least five full chambers, combined with five pulls of the trigger: one of which isn't attempted suicide, just self-dramatising stupidity.

I'm not sure if it should be a source of pride or shame, but Britain's Beachy Head, in East Sussex, has overtaken the Golden Gate Bridge in San Francisco as the world's number one destination for committing suicide. I had directions on a piece of paper which included the name of the last pub before the sheer-drop white cliffs – which stated opening hours and happy-hour prices – but I've bloody well lost it. If I were the hail-fellow-well-met landlord of this goldmine establishment I'd rename it 'The Last Jump Inn' and instead of free drinks for suicides I'd charge the contents of their wallets or purse (which would stop at least half of them in their solipsistic tracks I'm sure). Catering for coach parties of suicides would boost trade considerably, even if return business and word-of-mouth recommendation were limited. Edinburgh has 'The Bridges', but you run the risk of someone beneath the glass panes on a railway platform being killed by your plummeting body; there's also the Forth Road Bridge, but you run a small risk of surviving the fall and the water.

At least one of suicide's many advantages is not having to attend any more funerals (except your own). Hopefully if you've got the imagination and guts to commit suicide in all planned seriousness, you've got the good taste not to choose the most requested tune at British funerals – namely, 'I Will Survive' by Gloria Gaynor. Sorry, only kidding . . . It's actually 'I Will Always Love You' by Whitney Houston, the haunting theme from *The Bodyguard* movie, which also starred Kevin Costner, who from a recent appearance on the *Heaven and Earth Show* apparently believes that there must be something after death. Maybe not for all of us, but depriving Hollywood superstars of personal immortality would just be too cruel a trick by God (who gave them the faith in themselves and Him to become Hollywood superstars in the first place).

14. Korea Team Fighting Pole People

South Korea 2 Poland 0
Busan: Tuesday, 4 June, 12.30 p.m., BBC

Co-hosts South Korea had 45 minutes to digest Japan's 2–2 result against the Belgians before kicking off their sixth World Cup campaign – not having won a single game in the previous five. A score-draw was the benchmark to be measured against, because their northern European opponents were of a similar standard on paper. As mentioned Belgium had reached the semis in 1986, a feat Poland had achieved twice previously in 1974 and 1982. Belgium had of course suffered like all the occupied countries in the Second World War, but not as much as Poland, which lost over a fifth of its population. Again as previously stated, Korea had endured Japanese occupation and the horrors of the Korean War (a 'police action' which cost the lives of four *million* people – mostly Korean but including a sizeable number of casualties from China, America, Britain, Canada, Australia, Turkey and many others contributing to the UN forces). North and South are still technically at war and the De-militarised Zone stretches along the 38th parallel. North Korea is an economic developing-world kitten, whereas the South is an Asian tiger economy with a growth rate to match. South Koreans are the biggest Internet users in the world and they avoided the fiscal crash that heralded the end of the Japanese economic miracle. South Korean schoolchildren receive lessons in 'anti-communism' as well as English (since the Korean language is even more difficult for Westerners to learn than Japanese).

The Poles, would you believe, invented Esperanto, a possible reaction to jaws dropping at the length and consonant-heavy spelling of their surnames (examples from this year's crop of Polish pro-footballers including Krzynowek, Swierczewski and Kryszalowicz).

The Solidarity trade union applied some of the first pressure that led to the downfall of the Berlin Wall and for many Poles 1980–89 was a period of unmatched excitement, hope and prosperity. Electrician Lech Walesa started this decade in the Gdansk shipyard and ended it in the presidential palace (which is where the drinking and depression really began to affect his behaviour). Just before this match, the Polish government tried to introduce legislation to ban the import of second-hand clothing in order to try and save the ailing textile industry. The Polish team are a straight division of those labouring with Polish clubs and those lucky enough to be playing in Western European leagues.

Phew, a great big paragraph of socio-economic history which I'm sure you enjoyed reading as much as I disrelished writing it (but at least be grateful that you don't have to go back and type all those words, especially the Polish ones).

Poland had topped their qualifying group, a turnaround in form of 180 degrees that owed much to Nigerian-born striker Emmanuel Olisadebe of Panathinaikos, who coach Jerzey Engel helped gain citizenship a lot faster than your average black immigrant from Africa who finds himself looking for work in Warsaw (Olisadebe at the time turning out for Polonia Warsaw).

Guus Hiddink had been lured away from Holland to help South Korea put together a squad that could avoid being the first ever host nation to fall at the first fence of qualifying for the second round (a prospect that must have kept their organising committee chairman awake at night, only drifting into fitful sleep filled with nightmare scenario images of Japan succeeding in doing so). Warm-up games against strong opposition produced results that must have made Hiddink wish he'd lined up bounce games against teams of Seoul waiters or Incheon bar regulars. At least *one* victory in Group D was a political imperative, so that the Commie bastards over the border could no longer dismiss the 1988 Olympics in Seoul as less of an achievement than North Korea's win over Italy in a far away place called Middlesbrough 36 years previously. And the jumped-up Japanese had got off to a non-losing start.

If the atmosphere in Saitama had been pleasantly electric, the 60,000 in Busan generated a feeling in the humid air that was positively atomic. The home team at first struggled to harness the positive energy flowing in their direction and Olisadebe should have scored in the first minute. Hwang Sun-Hong made no mistake with his chance and the Busan Sports Complex Stadium almost went into China Syndrome nuclear meltdown. The Japanese had supported from their seats, the South Koreans were giving it laldy on their feet. At half-time, panellist Lawrenson described a replay of the celebrating fans as, 'The best crowd shot in the World Cup so far'. And so it was, two tiers full of South Koreans in their red replica shirts going gaga for their country.

In the second half, South Korea were unable to maintain such speed and pace – so they went into a higher gear and the Poles knew they couldn't stop them disappearing over the horizon of the winning line. Yoo Sang-Chul made it 2–0 and the blazered Hiddink was punching the air. Like Japan, but with more horsepower, South Korea's midfielders and forwards passed short, ran, collected and ran at their retreating opponents. If this was football Pacific Rim style, long may it continue to flourish (or at least until the latter stages). It literally gave me goosebumps and an adrenaline buzz.

15. Raiders of the Lost Empire

The old USSR reached the semi-finals in 1966, but as a capitalist democracy the Russians have continued to underachieve on the world footballing stage. Despite the collapse of communism, the Russian people continue to consume industrial quantities of the social lubricant vodka (the taxes on which paid every salary of Red Army employees during the Soviet era, with some revenue left over to pay for drying-out clinics – even if the level of luxury failed to match that of the Betty Ford Clinic or The Priory).

Tunisia may be nicknamed the Cinderella of North Africa, but it is one of the more desirable locations for newly born babies coming into the world via Africa. Olive oil is to Tunisians what vodka is to Russians, with the result that Tunisians are less likely to die prematurely of cirrhosis of the liver. Movie companies often use it for location shoots, examples including *Raiders of the Lost Ark*, *The Sheltering Sky* and *The English Patient* (whereas Scotland has to make do with *Rob Roy*, *Local Hero* and *Gregory's Girl*,[1] not even being able to boast about *Braveheart* since most of it was shot on location in Ireland!). The Tunisian team secured the first African victory in World Cup history, beating Mexico in 1978. However, prior to this World Cup they lost in quick succession a German and then a French coach. Poor Ammar Souayah got lumbered with the responsibility a few days before this kick-off. Russian coach Oleg Romantsev, on the other hand, had clocked up eight years in joint charge of the Russian squad and Spartak Moscow.

A 7.30 a.m. rise for this frankly unattractive fixture wasn't achieved without difficulty, although a bottle of olive oil instead of vodka the night before would have had me up in good time (if only to go to the bathroom with green diarrhoea), and I could have done without Bob Wilson as ITV's early-morning presenter. Prime-time anchor man Des Lynam presents with a sexy twinkle in his eye, as if having just finished dragging on a spliff during the opening credits, whereas Wilson hasn't unwoodenised an iota since his *Football Focus* apprenticeship in front of the cameras. His sidekicks for this milk-delivery time-slot were Bobby Robson and Ally McCoist and at one memorable point a Bob–Bobby exchange petered out into . . . *dead air*.

The game was a televisual waste of airspace, too, the Russians huffing and puffing for their two goals. Once again the Russians were sporting the worst haircuts in a tournament. I don't mean they turned out in a rash of Mohicans, dodgy dye-jobs or Number One skinheads, which had been disfiguring the competition up to this point, but that they looked like the male models who feature in photographs pinned to the walls of traditional barbers, circa 1975 – a gruesome mix of dreadful perms, blow-dried Jason Kings and schoolboy bowl-cuts.

It all made for desperately dull viewing, but the desire not to miss anything being broadcast had already led to at least two fatal casualties amongst the watching worldwide audience. A Turk had fallen down a ventilation shaft while adjusting an aerial, while a colour-blind Albanian had managed to electrocute himself while attempting to fix a loose wire in his TV set.

NOTES

[1] *The English Patient* is a terrific movie (but boring book). *Gregory's Girl* is a terrible movie. I once had a blazing row with a stranger on a Citylink coach about comparisons between *Gregory's Girl* and *St Elmo's Fire*. The congenital female idiot in the seat next to me cited *Gregory's Girl* as her favourite all-time movie and dismissed *St Elmo's Fire* as 'formulaic Hollywood drivel'. Bill Forsyth's breakthrough film is so bad that showing it ought to be made illegal in Scotland. It is badly directed, poorly written and appallingly acted. Writer-director Joel Schumacher's box-office hit had a great theme tune by John Parr, its Brat Pack stars could actually act and it constitutes 108 minutes of pure entertainment. If I want to watch a bunch of sad Scots embarrassing

themselves I'll buy a video camera and film my own life. The '*GG–SEF*' dichotomy is a personal test I use for rating people, and if anyone comes down wrong on *both* sides of the equation, I write them off as cultural dead wood.

16. A Paragraph in *USA Today*

USA 3 Portugal 2
Suwon: Wednesday, 5 June, 10 a.m., BBC

Portugal and Spain were the 15th-century equivalents of the USSR and the USA – an appropriate analogy because when the Portuguese overextended themselves with their vast empire, Spain was waiting to pick up the pieces. Today the USA is *numero uno* and reigns supreme and unchallenged (if misunderstood and unloved by its jealous enemies). Only 5 per cent of the world's population may be lucky enough to live there – a figure that would soon double/treble/quadruple if green cards were freely available to all-comers – but this economic and geographical giant of federated states consumes over 25 per cent of the world's resources.

Portugal produces all of the planet's port (for the uncultured palates of British pensioners) and three-quarters of all cork (for the wine industry which cannot overcome consumer resistance to plastic plugs or metal screw-tops, except in Britain where there really are best-selling supermarket wines called 'Old Git', 'Fat Bastard' and 'Cat's Piss'). The Portuguese still believe that they discovered America before Columbus (who understood the importance of publicity) and their famous sons Magellan and Diaz were world-class explorers (unlike the Big C, who once got lost and ran aground sailing between the Rock of Gibraltar and Algeciras on mainland Spain).

Despite America having 18 million registered players – c.f. Portugal's total population of just over 10 million – football in the USA still has a glitzy but ersatz feel about it (at least from a Euro-centric perspective). Even the terminology is grating to a soccer sophisticate from sunny Scotland – 'offense' and 'defense', 'out of bounds', 'overtime', 'assists', 'You were huge for the penalty, Brad', etcetera – as well as having bizarrely named team franchises in their semi-pro league, such as the San Francisco Earthquakes and the Kansas City Whizz. At grass-roots level, it is kept going by Hispanics, college students and soccer moms. Its middle-class status is obvious when you examine the racial make-up of the national squad, with its WASP members outnumbering African-American players like Demarcus Beasley. Blacks *are* American boxing, of course, and African-Americans dominate basketball and American football (if not quite baseball). Americans apparently prefer to boost home-town sports that were born in America, which is fine and good except when describing the final play-off games in baseball as 'the World Series'.

The American media just don't take soccer seriously, and even sportswriters who pride themselves on the quality of their prose and the breadth of their sporting knowledge would struggle to recall US soccer's greatest achievement: beating a full-strength England 1–0 in the 1950 finals. Goal-scorer Joe Gaetjens should be as famous as Joe Di Maggio, but instead of becoming a millionaire and marrying Marilyn Monroe he literally disappeared off the sporting radar and was never heard from again (after returning to Haiti and falling foul of the Ton Ton Macoute, who, quite seriously, had the contract for supplying all the baseballs that the US needed to import). US sportswriters are the best in the world, because they regard sportswriting and literature as co-operating team-mates not mutually-exclusive opponents, and their ranks have included writers like Ring Lardner, George Plimpton, Norman Mailer, Ernest Hemingway, Damon Runyon, A.J. Liebling and Thomas Boswell. Of course, the best *writers* in general are American and I could have added 'Frank Bascombe' to the above list, except that he is the literary creation of novelist Richard Ford and appears as the hero of *The Sportswriter* (the greatest novel ever written, and not just about sodding 'sportswriting', which the book is only about *ostensibly*).

Bascombe, the narrator, likens himself as a sportswriter to a travelling salesman, rather than bumming himself up as 'a genuine writer' – because even as a cut above 'a fly-swat reporter' (i.e. match-reporting hack) the genre offers little opportunity for real creativity. This argument may seem to be undermining my point, but that is the brilliance inherent in the idea of the novel, written by a literary genius.

At one point Bascombe even rejects the idea of sports as a metaphor for life, calling the commonly drawn connection 'pretty reductive'. He opines that, 'Life doesn't need a metaphor in my opinion.' I'm not relegating this paragraph to a fucking endnote, because my point is important and can be summed up thus: instead of buying another Nick Hornby novel – or even God forbid one by Ben Elton – go and buy a copy of *The Sportswriter*!

Because of 11 September, the US soccer squad were protected in South Korea like a collection of visiting ex-Presidents. Such security was also essential when the USA played Iran during France '98. That meeting of football lightweights was billed as an ideological grudge match, hyped up as Allah's Acolytes versus the Great Satan, but it was complete 'handbags' as Ron Atkinson would describe it. Iran won 2–1 in a match with about as much bite as a Soccer Moms' XI versus a Helen Keller School Select.

Led by Luis Figo, Real Madrid and Europe's second-best player, this Portuguese team were highly fancied dark horses; and their expectant public back home had just participated in a general election where football-related issues dominated (the main political bone of contention being planning permission for Benfica's new stadium, and whether the new government would foot the bill for building it). In Lisbon at least, Anton Oliveira's sleek caravel of superstars was expected to sail into Yokohama harbour for a Cup final showdown with whoever.

Team USA responded like pirates and brigands, clambering up and down the Portuguese man-o'-war's rigging before Captain Figo even had a chance to get his sails unfurled. Four minutes in and America were one up, after normally reliable Vitor Baia had fumbled fatally. Before the Group D favourites could draw breath and re-group, a cross deflected off Jorge Costa for a second, with Baia scrambling hopelessly. Charlton Athletic fans have christened Costa 'The Tank' and the lumbering defender was playing like one. Portugal were close to panic and soon began to lose their heads right, left and centre. The USA were punching so hard above their weight that the Portuguese players were looking dazed and confused. They began to weather the storm and a goal before half time would have restored some law and order to the unfolding riot of footballing anarchy. In the 36th minute a glorious diving header from Brian McBride of Columbus Crew (!) put the USA 3–0 up.

I was up out of my seat screaming, 'Go, USA, go!' (and I was *supporting* Portugal). The only Portuguese 'enjoying' this horror show were professional *fadistas*, or singing wailers who specialise in depressing diners in restaurants with the famous *fado* (plaintive ballads about lost love, money and hope). Figo just looked fagged out and extremely *fado*-ed (to put it mildly). If only the US could hold out until half-time, now that Portugal had at last realised they were sailing up shit creek without a paddle. A poor US clearance from a corner was collected by Beto and he side-footed past Brad Friedel. Blast, 3–1. This looked likely to be another 0–3 comeback as when Portugal eventually beat North Korea 4–3 in 1966.

In the second period – sorry, half – Portugal had the wind in their sails and the Americans were beginning to sink with fatigue. With 20 minutes left I was literally on my knees praying for America. Thirty-three-year-old Jeff Agoos sliced unstoppably into his own net.

'Goose, ya goddam schmuck!'

It had taken him 19 years since his debut cap to make it into a game at the World Cup finals and although he would only be famous for 15 minutes in America, he would be infamous throughout the rest of Planet Football for eternity if his side didn't hang on for an 'unbelievable' victory. As a pony-tailed, laid-back Californian I don't think he quite realised the significance of his spectacular strike.

America ran down the clock in the Portuguese corner flags but held out easily even when they lost possession. I couldn't have been more relieved for big Goosey if he had been a blood relation.

US coach Bruce Arena – a typically American name don't ya think? – looked understandably delighted. Barry Davies commented: 'Bruce Arena is in some sort of heavenly arena.'[1]

Back in the Beeb studio, professional *fadista* Alan Hansen summed up the biggest World Cup shock in decades: 'One paragraph in *USA Today*, if they're lucky.'

And so ended the first tranche of group games.

NOTES

[1] Bruce Arena couldn't be British, just as Barry Davies couldn't be American. Try and imagine a Yank called Nigel, Derek, Ian or Giles. Now try imagining a Brit named Dwight, Seymour, Duane or Sheldon . . .

17. Gob-smacked in Ibaraki

Germany 1 Republic of Ireland 1
Ibaraki: Wednesday, 5 June, 12.30 p.m., ITV

Guinness were running a commercial based around a Gaelic-football cup final, featuring a player about to take a potentially match-winning penalty (which involved tossing a small hard white ball in the air and giving it a lash with a stick). A commentating voice-over asked: 'What must be going through that young man's head? Will he be going home to a hero's welcome tonight?' The commercial, which had the production values of a Hollywood film and a similarly sentimental story narrative, then cut to the player being carried shoulder high into a bar, surrounded by supporters from the county of his birth. Whether this scene was an objective happy ending or just the player's hyperactive imagination was left ambiguously open. The director then cut to the white ball being tossed in the air . . .

The opposition had been portrayed as subjective projections of a worried mind, warrior wart-hogs lined up on the goal-line snorting and snarling, a not inappropriate comparison to draw with Rudi Völler's team, since the Germans had stopped playing for the sympathy vote and started reverting to arrogant type in the wake of the 8–0 thrashing of Saudi Arabia. They were walking tall once more, and facing an Irish team of unprepossessing physical specimens like the Saudis. Under Jack Charlton the Republic had played a hit-and-hope game, thumping long balls and even goal-kicks up the park to a big striker; under Mick McCarthy they had to adapt to having Michael Owen-sized forwards, which of course involved playing football out of defence. For this game, winger Jason McAteer was still injured and Steve Staunton was having to fill in at centre-half (and although 'Stan the Man' was collecting his 100th cap he was still significantly smaller than 6 ft–plus German *blunderbuss* Carsten Jancker). Irish eyes may have been smiling before kick-off, but even the most optimistic fan must have half-expected to be watching the conclusion to this match through gaps in tear-stained fingers.

For 20 long minutes the Germans swaggered and the Irish sweated. Klose scored with a fine header and indulged in another forward-flip to celebrate. With the BBC having secured the next two England games for exclusive broadcast, ITV were having to make do with live rights to the Irish games. Clive Tyldsley's sympathetic attitude to the boys in green was slipping a little and Damien Duff of Blackburn Rovers was described as not being a George Best. Thinking better of the unfair comparison, Clive skilfully retracted with the obvious observation that nobody else but George Best is. 'Different style, different Ireland...' The brilliant Ballack was so good that Clive found it hard to tell if he was right- or left-footed (much like Jancker – who, luckily for the Irish, air-footed a glorious chance to kill the game, since he seems equally bloody bad on either foot). After the goal the Germans withdrew into their own half (if only to keep the ball away from Jancker, who is as bald as he is bad but who managed to miss another sitter in the second half before being replaced by Bierhoff). Any quarter-chances for Ireland were snuffed out by keeper Oliver Kahn. The Germans continued to sit on their lead and close to the end were putting up their size-12 feet, swilling beer, eating Bratwurst, patting their ample stomachs and listening to James Last playing brass-band military swing on their Sony music systems (or at least their supporters back home were). Against the fighting Irish this is footballing suicide, psychological *kriegspiel* (a German variation of chess where you have no information about an opponent's position or movements except via a referee).

I wish I could say I was standing in front of the TV screaming '*Schlaraffenland*, Völler!' (or 'Fool's paradise, Rudi!'), but I was just disappointed and had given up all hope of seeing an equaliser. Even tall substitute Niall Quinn[1] had failed to stir things up in the centre of the rock-solid German defence – until the 93rd minute when Steve Finnan blootered a high punt into the so-far impregnable opposition box. Quinn jumped mightily, so to speak, and flicked the Fevernova on into space, where Robbie '*Wunderkind*' Keane of Leeds United got on the end of it. Awkward and off-balance, he controlled the ball with a thick thigh, with Kahn advancing like a Panzer and looming larger and larger by the nanosecond. Keano just got his shot away with Kahn almost on top of him.

Cut to a gob-smacked McCarthy in the technical area, his jaw dropping like a hanged man falling through dividing floorboards. It remained agape in pure amazement at what he was witnessing (one of the most striking, memorable and amusing visual images of this World Cup).

Kahn semi-smothered the shot but it spun up into the roof of the net. Keano celebrated with a secondary-school comprehensive somersault and a primary-school forward roll.[2]

The Guinness ad ended in dramatic slow motion, with the white ball spinning in the air and then being whacked. It finished there, with the harp company logo and the word: 'Believe'.[3]

NOTES

[1] Niall Quinn deserves at least an endnote for his contribution to charity before the tournament started. The 35-year-old veteran had a testimonial match in May 2002 but decided to give the proceeds of the Sunderland–Republic XI match to hospitals in Sunderland and Dublin, as well as a charity helping street children in Calcutta. If the fixture failed to raise the expected million pounds, he promised to fundraise to reach that total. Testimonials today are still tax-*free* sources of income, but are becoming increasingly rare and almost impossible to justify (because players rarely stay with one club for any length of time and are paid astronomical salaries into the bargain). Quinn's gesture was commendable even if he already is a millionaire (but not many of those would turn down the chance to double their money). Hopefully it will set a precedent – although I wouldn't put money on it.

[2] I have a genuine phobia when it comes to somersaults (which isn't quite as weird as Billy Bob Thornton's allergy to antique furniture and Benjamin Disraeli's hair). My fear stems from an incident in secondary-school gym class, where I volunteered to somersault over a vaulting horse (in order to impress a pretty teenage girl waiting to deliver a note to our sadistic P.E. teacher). My adolescent peers all had Adidas trainers and shop-bought

shorts; I had a pair of cheap black plimsolls and home-sewn shorts (which stopped not at my waist or belly-button but just below my nipples). I lost my nerve and after some bad-natured ribbing was told to go and shower for being such a big girl's blouse. On the way to the changing room I stopped to watch as my replacement pounded towards the gym horse. In mid-flip he lost his bearings and tried to abort the somersault. I'll never forget the sound of a neck breaking or spinal column snapping (although after hospital treatment he did walk again).

[3] Like rival brand Murphy's, I'm sure Roy Keane isn't bitter. Then again, one contributor to RTE's World Cup radio coverage broadcast from Dublin never got invited back after he suggested that his sources reliably informed him that Roy Keane was hating every minute of Ireland's success, because it was being achieved without him.

18. The *Bon*, the *Mauvais* and the *Laid*

Denmark 1 Senegal 1
Daegu: Thursday, 6 June, 7.30 a.m., BBC

Another star was born in this encounter, although his delivery into the public consciousness could be described as torturous. Salif Diao's equalising goal for Senegal was replayed at full-time from behind his keeper's goal, a terrific aerial shot with Diao's 90-yard sprint highlighted all the way by placing him in a lighted bubble against a darkened background. (It was an intriguing perspective, made possible by the robotic TV cranes positioned behind each goal and which swooped down towards the penalty-box action whenever a goal looked imminent). The wonderfully named Henri Camera had dispossessed Martin Jorgensen in the Senegalese 'D' and then short-passed to Diouf, who one-touched to Diao who then sent the ball forward and kept on running until the ball came back to him in the Danish penalty box, where he finished the move he had started by flicking it into the net with the outside of his boot. The lead-up work had been terrific and the finish was outstanding.

If his goal was the good, the bad had been his earlier tackle on Tomasson, which gave away a needless penalty and the lead to Denmark. And the ugly? Diao's tackle on Rene Henrikson was staggeringly unattractive, with studs bared and sinking sickeningly into shin bone. His straight-red dismissal probably deprived his on-top side of a deserved victory, as Denmark were visibly wilting in the 95-degree heat.

As for Morten Olsen's men, they had earned an ice-cold Carlsberg, who were running one of the best football tie-in commercials. In it a pub player fantasises about professional fame and fortune, imagining himself on the front page of *The Sun* as the first £100,000-a-week

British player and being photographed for the covers of *The Face* and *Hello!* magazines. (Note well that the mocked-up front page and covers were all those of *real* publications, not spoofs such as the *Daily Bugle*, *The Visage* or *Hi Baby!*) In his mansion in some stockbroker belt he is greeted by two cute blondes in riding outfits. The clever twist comes when he rings for service and the bell tinkling in the scullery interrupts the butler-cum-boot-boy cleaning his football boots with a toothbrush and polish – ex-player and high-profile pundit Alan Hansen (and the surname Hansen is as common in Denmark as Smith is in Britain).

'If we were football agents, we'd probably be the best football agents in the world.'

And we consumers can share the dream merely by purchasing a six-pack of Carlsberg Special Brew . . .

19. No 99-nil Thriller in Saitama

Cameroon 1 Saudi Arabia 0
Saitama: Thursday, 6 June, 10.00 a.m., ITV

A channel hop over to ITV for the mid-morning match, with presenter Bob Wilson and pundit Jimmy Floyd Hasselbank, football for breakfast, elevenses and lunch certainly beating the normal TV programming broadcast during these hours, but Bob and Jimmy's sparkling dialogue wasn't quite on the Jerry Springer/Oprah Winfrey level provided by the displaced *Kilroy* and *Trisha*. Both these shows were inspired by Jerry Springer's format and on BBC 1 ex-Labour MP Robert Kilroy-Silk could usually be relied upon to keep things moving along with the skilled sincerity of a snake-oil salesman, his audience/participants in the studio being a mix of C1 and C2s. On ITV 1, however, Trisha exhibited all the warmth of Lucrezia Borgia with a viper crawling into her vagina; but she did have to work with guests and audiences who barely qualified for the DE marketing classification. On *Kilroy* the subject of deceased grandmothers might be discussed, sensitively if superficially; on *Trisha* any such topic would be taken downmarket and transmogrified into: 'Would you rape your dead grandmother for her social security book?'

Three back-to-back international football matches were a big improvement in programming, although the note-taking I had to do throughout and the writing up from mid-afternoons onwards was slightly spoiling the spontaneity of my spectating pleasure.

Although football is only a game, even at the rarefied World Cup level, another 8–0 humiliation for the Saudis could have had some serious consequences – psychologically and politically. But football gives every team the opportunity to make a new start, since you're only as bad as your last game, and Saudi Arabia in their all-white change strip (from unlucky green) were obviously determined to regain some pride. They outplayed match favourites Cameroon and should have scored at least twice (but scoring goals is a lot harder than preventing them). Surprisingly Cameroon were just coming to the end of an eight-match winless streak in World Cup fixtures. Hence, their satisfaction at taking the lead and contentment to sit on it.

Samuel Eto'o of Real Mallorca was the hero for the Lions and he stripped off his shirt before running across the pitch for a hetero-erotic hug with coach Schafer – the German tactical genius with the non-haircut (and whose long blonde locks suddenly reminded me of actor Klaus Kinski). If Cameroon should go out, I thought, maybe he could lead his disappointed squad into the deepest jungles of this tropical country and do something Wagnerianly weird like build an opera house (which was the plot of a Wim Wenders movie starring a wild-eyed Kinski, I'm sure).

An action shot of Eto'o preparing to shoot just before his goal, which appeared all over the press the next morning, captured the classic pose of an athletic footballer on the top of his game – arms fully extended like wings and tilted at 22.5 degrees, head down, and right leg in a cocked-to-shoot position. The picture-editor numskull in my head couldn't help but compare it with Robbie Keane's captured-on-still-camera physical contortions when scoring his last-gasp equaliser, Keano resembling a hunchback with arthritis tripping over his own splayed feet.

I should perhaps add that Nawaf Al-Tanyat of Saudi Arabia was voted Man of the Match. Also, in Arabic there are apparently 99 words to describe God and I reckon poor old Saudi coach Nasser Al-Johar must have used most of them in his thank-you-very-much prayers. After all, against Germany his team had only equalled a score-line achieved previously by Bolivia (against Uruguay in 1950) and Cuba (against Sweden in 1938). Zaire had lost 9–0 to Yugoslavia in 1974 and El Salvador were still the all-time whipping boys with a 10–1 loss to Hungary in 1982. If anything, 0–1 was a moral victory of sorts for Saudi Arabia.

20. Charge of the Light *Bleu* Brigade

France 0 Uruguay 0
Busan: Thursday, 6 June, 12.30 p.m., BBC

Back to the BBC and everyone's favourite big brother, Gary Lineker, who was babysitting Hansen, O'Neill and the pram-rattling Reid. The pronunciation of 'Uruguay' was becoming a bone of contention between big Alan and little Martin (with attention-deficient Peter happy to suck his thumb and remain well out of it).

Patient, multilingual Gary settled the matter definitively, noting the Spanish stressor 'Oo' on the first syllable. Uncle Bob (Wilson) on ITV would have been reduced to a nervous wreck by this kind of live on air lesson in linguistics; and to be fair to Peter he was quite possibly living in dread at the prospect of having to make a stab at pronouncing 'Bixente Lizarazu' at some point. (It may be a sadistic fantasy, but I'd love to see Reid and Gazza as co-presenters of their own footie show, *à la Saint and Greavsie* and faced with a goal-scoring forward line of Nietzsche, Wittgenstein, Titian and Solzhenitsyn.)

French coach Roger Lemerre must have been concerned that he was following in the fatal footsteps of Robespierre. With the 1998 World Cup and Euro 2000 safely in the record books, as part of a footballing revolution as radical and exciting as those planned and executed by the likes of Brazil and Holland, surely things weren't about to go horribly wrong in the absence of Aimé Jacquet as coach? Defeat against equally pointless Uruguay and a first-round *sortie* would have had the French press and media and public sharpening their metaphorical guillotines.

Within 15 minutes Lemerre and France got a lucky break, when Frank Leboeuf was stretchered off. The operator of the hand-held camera on the touchline turned out to be the moonlighting director of the Impulse moisturising body spray commercial, but this time he didn't have to worry about the bourgeois bores on the Advertising Standards Authority with their updated Hays Code for the 21st century – namely no crotch shots. The next Truffaut or Godard was in there like *un whippet*, shooting fast and low, capturing the thick matted growth of Leboeuf's matt-black pubic hairs. A descending left testicle completed this gruesome picture, which when flashed up on the screens at either end of the stadium had the more sensitive Koreans keeling over. (Bizarrely, from the waist up Leboeuf is exfoliated to the point where his skin shines like a baby's bottom.) He was replaced by Vincent Candela,[1] a sub who hadn't been caught on camera taking out his penis and pulling back the foreskin – unlike the American Demarcus Beasley.

Ten minutes later Thierry Henry slid into Marcelo Romero with his studs showing. If Stanislavsky had asked the South American to react 'like a Renault Clio which has been hit by an 18-wheeler truck' Romero couldn't have impressed students of method acting any more than he did. With Henry red-carded, Romero was back on the road with barely a scratch. Emmanuel Petit really should have followed his team-mate off the pitch for elbowing Sed Abreu in the face, but referee Ramas Rizo bottled the decision.

Uruguay being Uruguay proceeded to get ten of their eleven men behind the ball, so that the French not only had a mountainous Eiger to climb but had to approach it by the North Face. When Recoba rounded Barthez and missed a gaping goal with his educated-to-PhD-level left foot, I did a little jig of delight.

Ten-man France in the second half went for the win, relying on Barthez to pull off the necessary saves when required, but Uruguay's cowardly hit-on-the-break strategy was implemented with dour determination. It was depressing but exciting viewing, like watching nine cavaliers with rapiers and daggers being repelled from battlements by ten roundheads with pistols and pitchforks.

Zou-Zou was a no-show again because of the troublesome hamstring injury, and at this point President Chirac should have ordered him home to Paris for emergency treatment at the American hospital, where they could have rebuilt his left thigh with Renault Clio technology.

All was not lost, however. The French were progressing on an upward curve results-wise, albeit shallow. A 2–0 win against Denmark and they would still escape Group A . . .

NOTES

[1] What is it about French names that makes them so damn, for want of a better word, sexy? Leaving aside their better-known names, their squad still contained *je-ne-sais-quoi* monikers such as Gregory Coupet, Philippe Christanval, Alan Boghassian and Christophe Dugarry. England, on the other hand, had clunking nomenclatures like Nigel Martyn, Gareth Southgate, Wayne Bridge, Wes Brown, Nicky Butt(!) and Robbie Fowler. Of course, if 'converted' into French they would sound a lot classier. In my case, David Bennie has a stop-start, gutturally harsh aural feel to it, but if I were Parisian say, I would find it a lot more attractive and flowing as it rolled off my tongue; *Da-veed Ben-ay*. Classy or what? In Japanese, I'm *Debbido Bennamu*. For the record my porn nom de plume is *Pierre McMillan* (a combination of first-loved pet and mother's maiden name). Or *Pierro MikkMullanu*.

21. Swedish Beak-tweakers Score Brace

Sweden 2 Nigeria 1
Kobe: Friday, 7 June, 7.30 a.m., ITV

In 1995 Kobe lost 6,000 citizens to the earthquake which devastated the city. At a cost of £163 million, the Wing Stadium was topped off in October 2001, as part of the city's rebuilding process. A crowd of 36,194 left almost 6,000 empty seats. How much is an individual life worth? Using the above figures, one could do a back-of-envelope calculation and say £27,000 (approximately). As with the victims of the Twin Towers, who amounted in total to about 3,000 dead, I suppose insurance actuaries had to work out a monetary value for the earthquake victims, based on insurance policy premiums and small-print exclusions (such as 'acts of God'). Although the grief for family members and other loved ones must have been much the same, having someone die in a building that is destroyed by a natural disaster must be somewhat easier to bear than living with the thought that your deceased loved one was murdered by other human beings who didn't care who or how many they killed (including themselves). Whether facing kamikaze pilots in the Pacific Theatre of the Second World War or suicide-bombers hijacking civilian airliners from a New York City airport, the Western mind positively baulks at the thought processes required to carry out such acts. Many Americans, for example, sacrificed themselves in conscious acts of bravery to save fellow comrades during the Second World War, as well as facing the probability of death in order to kill as many of the enemy as possible, but orders to fly Mustangs straight into aircraft-carriers of the Imperial Japanese Navy would quite rightly have resulted in mutinous refusal. Flying say 40 'suicidal' sorties or missions against heavily defended enemy positions is one thing; flying one *suicidal* mission with no chance of return quite another. Even Timothy McVeigh who blew up the government building in Oklahoma is *just* within the bounds of psychological understanding – on a theoretical, abstract, impersonal level at least – since he didn't detonate the fertiliser truck while sitting suicidally in the driver's cab (although he did have to face capital punishment when apprehended and put on trial). Palestinian suicide-bombers, on the other hand, don't just kill innocent civilians in pizzerias, discos and bus-stations, they also destroy themselves in the murderous process. Without wishing to seem facetious about the wickedness involved in acts of terrorism, the US drama 24 is an interesting case in point. Made before but broadcast after 11 September, some scenes had to be re-edited in the wake of the New York tragedy, mostly concerning an airliner which is blown up in mid-air. The female terrorist accomplishes her foul deed after having parachuted out of the plane, and it explodes as she floats down to earth with a satisfied smirk on her face. Pre '9/11' this was a comprehensible if evil act. If she had been intent on blowing herself up with her victims, a script conference would have been hastily arranged and a script-doctor paged a.s.a.p. The FBI may well have missed clues about the planned attack on the Twin Towers and Pentagon, but if, as has been reported, a ground agent in Kansas sent in a report red-flagging the danger, his superiors can hardly be blamed if the suicidal self-immolating aspect of the plan caused them to shy away from the idea, like a horse refusing a water-jump . . . Human beings of whatever race, creed or religion have more in common than not, but Western materialism/secularism/nationalism is definitely a dividing factor when it comes to taking others down with oneself for a 'religious' cause (no matter how objectively or ostensibly 'noble').

On a more uplifting note, Sweden–Nigeria as an early-morning aperitif for the Big Game five hours later was a lip-smacking cocktail for footballaholics. The Super Eagles of Nigeria had been squabbling over bonus money for progressing in the tournament, but another defeat would have clipped their wings permanently. Austin 'Jay Jay' Okacha of Paris St Germain floats up and down a football pitch like an unfettered Golden Eagle, but in the dressing room squawks in repeated complaints like an irritating parrot. Freddie Ljungberg of Arsenal and Henrik Larsson of Celtic are the 'love-birds' of the

Swedish public (Freddie sporting a nest of red henna and Henrik having shaved off his crowning glory completely). At Arsenal, Freddie is part of an all-star cast, while at Celtic Henrik stands out like a budgerigar amongst sparrows (and although Johan Mjalby is a club and national team-mate, his play can be likened to that of a dodo bird or ostrich).

Nigeria took the lead through Julius Aghahowa – who must curse the trade winds that dumped him down in the Ukraine, playing for Shakhtar Donestsk – heading home after the Swedish back-four and goalkeeper did their famous 'We are ostriches with our heads in the sand' impersonation. The Super Eagles were finally flying and Freddie and Henrik were playing as if tied together by a long rope.

Freddie slipped his tethers with a Made-in-Highbury through ball. Henrik collected it, dropped a shoulder, shimmied and slotted home a Celtic-copywrighted goal – 1–1. In the second half Henrik 'Michael Owened' a penalty award in his dubious favour but didn't make a 'Gareth Southgate' of the conversion. Out came the tongue in celebration, an anatomical appendage that Celtic fans have grown to know and love (and if his other male member is in direct proportion *re* length and girth it would explain Mrs Larsson's permanent-seeming smile).

Jay Jay danced his way through half the Swedish team before finishing lamely. Left-back Teddy Lukcic prepared to blooter the ball to safety, with Celtic centre-half Mjalby lumbering back to 'help' but staggering across Lukcic's projected parabola for the ball. The Fevernova cannoned off Mjalby's shin and bobbled towards goal. When it hit the post and rebounded the heart went right out of the Super Eagles.

'Stand up if you hate Norway,' chanted the Swedish fans (in English), resulting in vertical viewers from Stavanger to Tromso (since no one loathes Norway like Norwegians, which is a Swedish folk-saying).

Nigeria would definitely be flying home after the England game.

22. How Senor Nadal Saved My Life

Spain 3 Paraguay 1
Jeonju: Friday, 7 June, 10 a.m., ITV

Despite Paraguay turning out in change strip of garish gold, the numskulls in my head whose unskilled and *temporary* job it was to keep me awake between 7.30 a.m. and 2.30 p.m. went on wildcat strike (citing compulsory and unpaid overtime). I shouldn't complain, really, since the erectile-function numskulls have been 'working-to-rule' for months, which is no fun when you're trying to run a body in difficult erotic conditions and the price of pornography is an inflationary nightmare.

I missed the own goal that put Paraguay one up, but woke up in time to see a couple of headers from Fernando Morientes and a penalty from Hierro seal the game for Spain. With Chilavert back from suspension, the eccentric goalkeeper had one dangerous free kick saved well by his opposite number Iker Casillas (and Chilavert's critics should note that he has a better record of goal-scoring per attempt than David Beckham or the vastly over-rated Roberto Carlos).

By full-time I was in danger of nodding off again, disappointed not to have seen Gaizka Mendieta get a game (his £20 million-plus transfer from Valencia to Lazio having turned into a loss-of-form nightmare). Since the summer of 1999, however, he no longer qualified as my favourite Spanish player, when I switched allegiance to the ageing and unglamorous stopper Miguel Angel Nadal (of Real Mallorca and ex-Barcelona) – because of his surname, however, not because of his nickname: 'The Beast'.

In Majorca for a few days to pay homage at the final resting place of Robert Graves, who is buried in the village of Deia, I was caught short on my travels by a debilitating migraine in the town of Soller, which according to my *Rough Guide to Spain* had no hostels or even hotels. Staggering down an unlikely looking side-street in the mid-day sun, I found myself in a car park cul-de-sac feeling dizzy and nauseous. Backtracking, the Hostal Nadal appeared as if from nowhere in my hour of real need. After checking in I swayed down a narrow corridor to my allocated room, which contained three single beds. After dry-swallowing four Nurofen-Plus I flopped onto the bed nearest the shuttered window. Eight hours' sleep saw me waking refreshed, the blinding headache not having developed into 48 hours of non-stop vomiting. I opened the shutters expecting a view of dustbins and/or a brick wall for my meagre eight pounds a night. Instead, dusk was falling over the Puig Major mountain, the highest peak on the island. Directly beneath my open window were sweet-smelling orange and lemon groves. I was one happy and relieved migraineur.

I don't know if Miguel Angel is related to the Nadals of Soller, or even if the family running this establishment were actually Nadals themselves, but the friendly proprietor made my stay a pleasure. Finding it may not have saved my life, literally speaking, but if I hadn't chanced upon the Hostal Nadal I still dread to think what might have happened to me. I'd have ended up in jail (as a suspected Scottish 'drunk') or in hospital (with an unpayable bill).

23. Boy David Plus Penalty Equals King David

Argentina 0 England 1
Sapporo: Friday, 7 June, 12.30 p.m., BBC

A second, unexpected verse of 'God Save the Queen' sent an unexpected, and frankly unwelcome, tingle down my spinal cord (and left the England players lip-synching to unlearned lyrics). David Beckham's swept up, spiky plume of a hairstyle had a lot resting on it, symbolically. It would be ridiculed mercilessly as a fashion *faux pas*, an adolescent affectation, if things went wrong; or it would be hyperbolically compared to the haircuts sported by the Minoan youths depicted on Grecian urns, doing somersaults over charging bulls, if everything went well . . .

Four years ago in St-Étienne, 'hard man' Diego Simeone had ruffled boy David's golden locks, a calculated wind-up which succeeded in bringing smarting tears of frustration to the 23-year-old's baby-blue peepers. Twenty-eight-year-old Simeone then decked the young pretender, who couldn't resist responding with his now infamous 'flick'. As a typically perfidious Latin, or cleverly cynical professional captain, Simeone staggered backwards and collapsed, writhing in pseudo-pain as if he were Caravaggio and had just been stilettoed in the calf by would-be assassins. As an example of win-at-all-costs thinking, it was a training-gound paradigm; as an act of sportsmanship it was spoliative, to put it mildly. Yes, young Becks had been guilty of petulance and immaturity, and technically he did deserve to be red-carded for 'physical retaliation'. Indeed, he almost certainly cost England the game – and theoretically could have been responsible for depriving his country of a second World Cup – but the recriminations that he had to endure for at least two seasons were grossly out of proportion, violently vicious and potentially crushing.

An inherent lack of intelligence and imagination may have helped him to cope psychologically, along with an obviously loving and supportive family, but Beckham had to pay a very high price for his mistake, at a usurious rate of payback interest. If character is destiny, his momentary weakness had set in motion a tide of events that could easily have overwhelmed a weaker personality. Even before the 2002 re-match, however, his destiny had been turned around in the right direction, upwards and onwards not downwards and backwards, and even an indifferent performance and result against Argentina would not have altered the rising trajectory of fame and fortune. Which made his decision to risk all in the course of the game all the more remarkable – and admirable.

Poet Sven had implored his players to find 'spirit stretching to the stars' (an exhortation which had left Gazza, in the ITV studio, strangely unmoved), but rocket-scientist Eriksson was still burning the midnight incense in search of a formula that would result in take-off and escape velocity being achieved against arch-rivals Argentina. Heskey was moved up front and the midfield strengthened.

For about 20 minutes, Argentina looked ominous, England adequate and Italian referee Pierluigi Collina increasingly like Max Schreck's *Nosferatu*. If Sven had been covering all the bases by taking a Fevernova ball and bouncing it off the head of a Buddhist statue, setting it alight in a Shinto temple, declaiming to it with Confucius-isms, christening it in a church with Volvic mineral water, circumcising it in a synagogue with a Swiss Army knife and finally kicking it away in the direction of Mecca from the top of a mosque's minaret, his ecumenical approach certainly paid off – for the footballing gods decided to intervene (maybe even because Ulrika had put in a good word with goddess Hera, protector of women and marriage, recommending Sven's cunnilingual dexterity and confirming his conjectured marriage proposal).

The ineffectual and overawed Owen Hargreaves injured himself in a collision with Michael Owen and couldn't continue. His obvious replacement would have been the untried Joe Cole, but the West Ham winger had himself been injured in training. This left third-choice Trevor Sinclair, who had been flying back and forth between London and Tokyo as a 'needed-not-needed-*needed*' last-minute replacement for the squad. When he came on, playing wide on the left, Paul Scholes moved infield to accommodate him and . . . everything *clicked* into place. The final small piece of the jigsaw had transformed the overall picture, and the Argentines couldn't have been more confused if they had been confronted by a canvas painted by M.C. Escher (with its optical illusions, dimensional shifts and mathematical tessellations – and I'm not sarcastically referring to a defence with Sol Campbell, Rio Ferdinand, and Danny Mills). Terrible football in the second half against Sweden had been transformed into . . . well, triumphant football, really.

Within minutes of the inspirational/responding-to-events substitution, Owen was off running at the retreating Argentina defence. Forty-two thousand spectators under the Sapporo Dome had flashbacks to his glory goal against the Argies in France '98 and little Michael must have had one too, because suddenly he was running in psychological sand. He got his shot away, nutmegging Walter Samuel in the process. The ball rebounded from the post.

It was all England now as Argentina struggled to stay in touch. Petrified by memories of the run-and-score Liverpool striker, Mauricio Pochettino stuck out a leg in panic a minute before half-time and Owen made absolutely sure he fell over it. Owen would have taken the penalty himself if not for the intervention of his courageous captain.

I watched intently as Beckham assumed an awesome responsibility. With his personal history in this explosive fixture, no one would have blamed him if he had hidden behind the convenient excuse of a suddenly troublesome metatarsal. But no, he was going to face down his mental demons, knowing that if he blinked they could destroy him . . . His nemesis Simeone got in on the dramatic act, too, trying to psyche Beckham out by offering a handshake (*the bastard*). After placing the ball on the spot, Beckham looked awfully young, visibly nervous and rather scared. He also appeared determined, decisive and detached. This was an all-or-nothing moment, put-all-my-winning-chips-on-black-please soccer roulette. Score and he would be a national hero, redeemed and adored. Miss and he would be a national disgrace again, reviled and abhorred. I was almost hyperventilating as he started his run-up . . .

'Come on, David! Come on, son . . . Yesssssssssssssssssssss!'

As penalty kicks go, it was actually rather poor. Eminently saveable in fact. But Pablo Cavallero had moved slightly to his right and his left foot was firmly planted and unmoving as the Fevernova missed hitting it by a foot or so. If Cavallero had remained stationary and standing upright he could have saved Beckham's effort by merely sticking out his left foot, casually and contemptuously. But he hadn't . . . And Beckham hadn't scuffed his shot or bottled his intention to hit the ball hard and straight.

'Character is destiny!' I shouted, enjoying Beckham's understandably ebullient celebrations. Although I was wearing my England top, it was white and I didn't feel compelled to pull it out of my waistband and kiss it (like Becks did with his red shirt; and the monetary value of this piece of footballing memorabilia – 'the Number 7 jersey Beckham wore when taking *that* penalty' – probably started growing exponentially the moment he kissed the three lions).

In the second half, England continued living in Svenland, one 17-pass move ending with a spectacular Teddy Sheringham volley which almost decapitated Cavallero. It was Total Football played by white Brazilians. Eventually Argentina rallied and for the final ten minutes they exerted a degree of control, but there was only one genuinely heart-stopping moment, when David Seaman had to block on his goal-line. As the minutes ticked by and my blood pressure rose, I realised I was *really* rooting for England, straight up and no jesting, mate, and only as the final seconds stretched out 'unbearably' did I remember my wager on Sven's men for the World Cup . . . It might not be fame and fortune, but watching your new favourite team playing fantasy football which if maintained could end with you pocketing a few hundred quid, wasn't a bad feeling . . .

The English media were of course in un-shut-uppable hyperdive mode – and why not? Bringing the BBC highlights show to a conclusion – after ITV had cleared their schedules for an 'as live' full-length re-run of the game at 8 p.m. – Lineker reviewed the first-edition front pages. 'Up yours, Señors!' *The Sun* had gone for, to which Lineker couldn't resist responding with: 'Up yours, *Señores*, actually.' Nobody likes a smartass, Gary, but Lineker is so tongue-in-cheek likeable that he gets away with it. He's developed so far and so quickly as a TV presenter that he could easily switch to *Newsnight Review* on BBC 2, fronted by witty and erudite Mark Lawson (who is *nothing* like Mark Lawrenson – and I don't just mean in physique). This arts review programme actually had a highbrow feature on 'football language in the media' called 'The Zen of Sven', which was reasonably entertaining and informative (unlike Gabby Yorath's sad spoof of the *Newsnight Review* piece on ITV, which involved getting Ally McCoist and Robbie Earle to wax philosophical about Wittegenstein and Nietszche *et al.* while sneaking embarrassed looks at an autocue or dummy board).

Watched live as sport, this game was exciting and dramatic; as a topic of conversation and discussion, it is now a shared cultural memory. Never mind President Kennedy or John Lennon being shot, for Brits over 15 the question is now: 'Where were you when Beckham scored the penalty against the Argies?' The phenomenon that is David Beckham will continue to grow and he is now world famous everywhere except America. He is footballing royalty, having proved himself to be not only a better footballer than Simeone but a bigger man as well. In fact, without exaggerating grossly, you could say he stepped out underneath the Sapporo Dome as a boy and walked off at full-time a king.

At the end of the game, the Argentines refused to swap jerseys. As David Beckham trotted happily towards the tunnel I was back on my feet, shouting the line Nick Carroway delivers to Jay Gatsby: 'You're worth the whole damn bunch of them put together!'

24. Bafana Bafana, Zlatko and Srecko

South Africa 1 Slovenia 0
Daegu: Saturday, 8 June, 7.30 a.m., ITV

The second set of matches in qualifying-group round-robins can be deathly dull affairs, and I knew I'd never be able to get up for this fixture (so I didn't go to bed and watched it drunk). Goal-scorer Siyabonga Nomvete was left unmarked by the (hungover?) Slovenian defence as early as the third minute and the way he converted Quinton Fortune's hanging cross suggested he'd been out on the razzle in downtown Daegu the night before – bending his neck to head home but instead 'thighing' the ball past Marko Simennovic. Benni McCarthy of FC Porto missed a couple of equally good chances. Still, Bafana Bafana and the rainbow nation of South Africa had won their first ever match in a World Cup tournament.

First-time participants Slovenia still hadn't, of course, and the pressure was getting to coach Srecko Katanec, who was red-carded for arguing with a FIFA official on the touchline. The poor man had broken down in tears and walked out of the first press conference after the first defeat to Spain and his 'controversial' substituting of our friend Zlatko Zahovic. Apparently, Zlatko had threatened to *buy* Srecko's home town – some little village in the Alps – and do what, I wondered, knock it down or impose a life ban on Zlatko ever returning? 'Everything that happened in the dressing room was out of normal human sense,' Srecko was quoted as saying. Benfica-bound Zlatko responded with Cantona-esque brevity and opaqueness: 'Whoever digs the hole often falls into it themselves.'

Who the hell do Slovenia think they are – Scotland?

25. An Archetypal or Typical Italian Performance?

Italy 1 Croatia 2
Ibaraki: Saturday, 8 June, 10 a.m., BBC

Gary Lineker summed up the Italian performance as 'archetypal'. A non-vocalised 'Eh?' crossed my mind and David O'Leary, as that morning's studio guest, paused momentarily before agreeing, 'Yes, a typical Italian performance, Gary.' Could Gary actually be angling for a move to arts or current affairs? As a successful England striker he had never been booked, never mind red-carded. As a blossoming television presenter he deserved a pat on the back from his producer for his quip about Jurgen Klinsman, who had accused Michael Owen of diving. 'A case of Herr Kettle calling the pot *Schwarz*, I reckon.' Brilliant line or what (even if it had been fed to him via his earpiece and then delivered deadpan).

Losing a 1–0 lead could be described as being *atypically* Italian, with their reputation for closing up shop successfully when the minimum necessary work to win has been completed, but snatching defeat from victory was typical in as much as modern Italian teams always seem to get into slow-starting trouble in the group stages of major competitions. This result, however, was more analogous to a high-speed car crash on the *autostrada* leading to Yokohama. Chain-smoking coach Trapattoni looked in need of an *ambulanza* by the end, for a suspected *attacco cardiaco* (especially when Totti saw a free-kick hit the base of a post and somehow spin along the goal-line without going in, with Italy still trailing).

Vieiri had given the Azzuri a deserved lead in the second half, but thereafter the Italians started to become paranoid about the dubious offside decisions being awarded against them. Instead of checking their runs slightly – to ensure another 'goal' wasn't chalked off –

English referee Graham Poll became the centre of a conspiracy theory.

The Croatians then helped themselves to two late goals, the first a gift due to non-existent marking and the second a fluke as Milan Rapaic's sliced and deflected shot spun over a helpless Gianluigi Buffon (a goalkeeper's name that is just asking for sub-editorial trouble). Filippo Inzhagi equalised with seconds to spare, but his subtle shirt-tug on Dano Simic was spotted by the Danish linesman.

The histrionic Italian protests were archetypal. Or typical. But equally pointless. At the final whistle the Croats grinned sheepishly and the Italians scowled wolfishly. Trapattoni's Italian tank was now running backwards, through all the reverse gears.

26. Peking Ducks Routed by Rio-lickin' Chickens

Brazil 4 China 0
Seogwipo: Saturday, 8 June, 12.30 p.m., ITV

Only 15 minutes in and China were starting to count their chickens. They gave away a free-kick 30 yards out and showed scrutable fear as Roberto Carlos lined up to take it. His PR people must be good because he hadn't actually scored from a dead-ball situation for his country since 1997! (In *Le Tournoi de France*, Roberto Carlos hit the memorable banana-bender that has resulted in his reputation as being 'deadly' from spot kicks.) The Chinese wall was a man short at one end and Carlos just blasted the ball phenomenally hard and completely straight. It soared into the far corner, leaving Jiang Jin in goal counting his first unhatched chicken. China lost two more goals before the break – but only one after the restart. Despite Zhao Junzhe managing to hit the Brazilian post near the end, the Chinese fans were actually getting *angry* at the 4–0 score-line and their team's poor showing. A few hats were thrown onto the pitch in disgust, probably belonging to demon gamblers who had put their monthly cash handout for having only one child on '3–0' or even '3–1' at the local bookies. Brazil were finger-lickin' good to watch and China were going home to count their ducks in terms of points and goals after playing Turkey.

27. Is Garth Crooks Speaking Mexican or Ecuadorian?

Mexico 2 Ecuador 1
Miyagi: Sunday, 9 June, 7.30 a.m., BBC

Yawn . . . I was struggling to release bladder muscles while listening to John Motson's commentary through two open doors – and hoping that the taste of blood in my mouth wasn't going to be reflected in my urine stream. *Here we go . . . Seems all clear . . . SHIT, a goddam goal . . . Bladder-muscle anchors on NOW! Dribble, dribble, dribble . . .*

Good old boy Ulises de la Cruz had sent over a decent cross for Ecuador striker Augustin Delgado to head home.

Images of champagne-and-croissant breakfasts had given way to the reality of early-morning punishment viewings, with your author unshaven, unshowered and half asleep . . . For a good few minutes I was left wondering why the Republic of Ireland were playing, confused by the green shirts of Mexico (and the olive-toned skin of their players). I missed Jared Borgetti's equalising goal, too, because of another unscheduled bathroom break (chronic constipation having turned into acute diarrhoea).

The winner came in the second half, when I was awake enough to appreciate it, Mexico's skin-headed midfielder Gerardo Torrado steaming through to score with an unstoppable shot. So, for once Mexico had managed to string together two consecutive World Cup group wins.

And at least the mid-morning game was on ITV, which meant no more in-stadium-situ interviews conducted by ex-footballer Garth Crooks. If Garth had a self-deprecating sense of humour he'd be dangerous. He sounds like an escapee from Broadmoor who has nevertheless completed his sociology degree from the Open University. A producer might whisper into his earpiece something about 'Out of sight, out of mind' but in Garth's mind this would be converted into a quote about: 'Invisible maniac'. Like a computer translating Spanish idioms into English, Garth's overly articulate pronunciation cannot compensate for a complete lack of coherent content. He may be syntactically correct but he's semantically meaningless.

'So, Debbido Beckham, if I may compliment you on your zero degree of haircut . . . as the match-winner by score goaling . . . given the circumstances of . . . the given conditions . . . could you comment on the metaphysical, metaphorical, even meteorological conditions and consequences of playing inside, even under, the Sapporo Dome . . .

'Thank you, David, for being interviewed by me. And now back to the studio.

'Hello, is that my line producer, Tristram, there? Look, Dahlink, I have to appear nude next time, because the integrity of my script demands it, that's why. I object to being called a complete *dingleberry* – which is a small faecal remnant attached to the hirsute growths around an anal entrance. Oh, alright then: a piece of shit on an arse hair! Hello, hello, hello?'

28. 'It's All Going Off . . .'

Costa Rica 1 Turkey 1
Incheon: Sunday, 9 June, 10.00 a.m., ITV

Gabby Logan was ITV's secret sexual weapon in the TV-ratings war with Auntie Beeb, but maybe because she is the daughter of ex-pro footballer Terry Yorath, she is a perfectly competent sportscaster. For the World Cup, however, ITV relegated her to the 'Naughty Corner', where you could cut the erotic tension between her, Ally McCoist and Andy Townsend with an industrial chainsaw. For the competition Hazel Irvine had only filed a few short pieces on film from Japan, one of which involved her tiptoeing into a hot spring clad only in a short towel (and if ITV ever succeed in poaching her I wouldn't put it past their production team to try and get her and Gabby wrestling together in a mud-bath). Another 'Ron-glish' feature deconstructed the term 'Handbags' (at ten paces), which a sheepish-looking Ron Atkinson at least admitted wasn't his concoction (or even football specific!).

As the teams walked out, Peter Drury informed us that the Turks had got their retaliation in first this time by complaining about the match referee *before* kick-off. They didn't care for the fact that Coffi Codja hailed from Benin, which doesn't have a professional league. It does have a population of four million, is the home of voodoo and has a capital city called Porto Novo. Despite taking the lead through Emre Beloziglu of Inter Milan[1], the Turks repeated the denouement of their Brazilian game, losing a late goal (to substitute Winston Parks).

Beloziglu in particular reacted like the head guard in *Midnight Express*, rushing into the Costa Rican technical area to push over an official retrieving the match ball (who thankfully didn't end up with a coat-hook spearing the back of his skull). Nevertheless, all the officials and both teams got involved in the 'handbags' mêlée which followed.

'It's all going off!' said an excited Drury. But disappointingly it didn't. Order was restored and Beloziglu booked.

Either Drury or co-commentator David Pleat left us with the observation that 'games are made up of moments'. Indeed. As is life. Some of which are *pivotal*.

NOTES

[1] All these 'wee diddy countries' with players registered with the likes of Inter Milan made me wonder . . . In the case of Beloziglu, he hadn't even started a game for the Italian giants in Serie A since his transfer from Galatasaray.

29. Zoom Football from Troussier's Samurai

Back to Auntie Beeb and bloody Barry Davies on microphone duty (ably assisted by anaemic Trevor Steven): 'Japan in yellow . . . To reiterate the colours. Russia in white, Japan in blue, and the Russian goalkeeper in *yellow* . . .' Good grief, does the rule about never apologising and never explaining apply to Davies?

Possibly because the Costa Ricans had suffered really bad haircuts at the hands of non-Spanish-speaking South Korean barbers, the Russians weren't willing to risk their fashion-plate feather cuts to the vagaries of Tokyo's hairdressing professionals, which was probably sensible considering the tonsorial misadventures of high magnitude that their Japanese opponents were sporting – including Number One skull-scrapers, more schoolboy bowl-cuts and fright-wigs with blonde and red dye jobs.

Davies drew our viewing attention to the different looks favoured by the two coaches. Philippe Troussier, even at 47, supposedly looked young enough 'to work in a bank checking spreadsheets for clients, whereas [Oleg] Romantsev [looked] as if he's been through the mill in football terms'. Troussier did look New Labour smart in a Hugo Boss or Paul Smith boxy suit, with shoulder-length hair and deconstruction spectacles. The bearded Rasputin-like character constantly at his elbow was apparently his French–Japanese interpreter (one Florent Dabadier, editor of the Japanese edition of *Premiere*). Romantsev had encased his not inconsiderable bulk in polyester and seemed to be internalising 'technical-area rage'.

Again, the home crowd were vocally hysterical, more like teenagers attending a pop concert than your typical football crowd. The Russian players were all big bastards, the Japanese just wee guys – like vodka-abuse survivors playing the vertically inconvenienced. This was another clash of footballing cultures, with the Russians throwing their weight around and the Japanese trying to play in top gear all the time.

In the second half, the Japanese became more menacing, both speeding up and becoming more accurate with their short-passes into space. It was a strange, exhilarating style, similar only to the South Koreans in this tournament, a sort of soccer *sancta simplicitas*. Or 'zoom football'. In response, the Russians were playing like a farm collective in the old USSR – a collective that wasn't hitting its quotas.

In 51 minutes, Arsenal misfit Inamoto beat an offside appeal and digging the ball out from slightly behind him shot unstoppably into the roof of the net. Seventy thousand home fans screamed, put their hands in the air and shouted in unison: 'Banzai . . . Goorul' A guest appearance from Elvis Presley at a Tokyo West Life concert couldn't have generated more squealing excitement. The zoom football continued to roar down the pitch, with Nakata determined not to be upstaged by Inamoto. His 30-yard shot rattled the crossbar with Rouslan Nigmatullin almost soiling his tracksuit bottoms in fright. The LOC family were edging towards Romantsev with their stretcher, since his impassive visage indicated a degree of suppressed anger that could have brought on a brain embolism. Instead he threw on sub Vladimir Beschastnykh, who slipped past stranded keeper Seigo Narazaki and with an open goal to walk the ball into blasted into the side-netting. The LOC family had to be physically restrained by FIFA officials as they tried to pull Romantsev into an oxygen tent.

At full-time, the stands of Yokohama's International Stadium were a sea of blue replica shirts, a positive kaleidoscope of colour (*pace* John Motson's description of yellow-shirted Brazilian fans). As the camera scanned round the celebrations, Davies failed to identity the VIP in the main stand, verbally confirming his lack of knowledge. It was only the Prime Minister of Japan (who Motty probably knew the name of).

Like the Ewoks in *Star Wars*, or the wee hooded scavengers scrambling over Rick Deckard's car in *Bladerunner*,[1] the LOCs made a final attempt to get Romantsev into intensive care, but he was to remain in a fatalistic condition for the rest of the tournament. Most of the crowd must have piled into trains for the short trip back to Tokyo, with Japanese National Railways having taken on extra 'professional pushers' for the evening to squeeze them in. The Russian players probably hit the nearest Yokohama bars for neat vodka self-medication, the Japanese heroes 24-hour hairdressing salons in the capital.

Sadly, after watching the defeat on a wide-screen television next to Red Square, 400 Muscovites rioted, killing one fan and injuring 100. Cars were ignited, shops looted and Japanese music students and tourists beaten up. Real enmity still exists from the sinking of the Russian Baltic fleet in 1905 by Japan and the two countries never formally sued for peace after the Second World War.

NOTES

[1] *Bladerunner's* Los Angeles of 2019 had the look of Tokyo 2002, and I saw this 1982 movie three times in three days when it was first released in Britain. It resulted in the worst haircut of my life, when I went into a fashionable unisex salon in Glasgow's Great Western Road with a publicity still of Harrison Ford from the movie. 'Give me a Rick Deckard like that,' I demanded, despite the polite protestations from my stylist that my hair was too fine and straight to be cut that short. I was quite pleased with the result in the full-length mirror until I put my spectacles back on, when I had to blink away tears while pretending to be delighted. In retrospect I looked as if I'd been given an 'Oleg Romantsev'.

30. Sun People Ying, Ivy Leaguers Yang

South Korea 1 USA 1
Daegu: Monday, 10 June, 7.30 a.m., ITV

Without air support, Bruce Arena's shock troops must have feared being overwhelmed by Guus Hiddink's guerrilla fighters (and the Taegu Sports Stadium's 60,000 red-shirted supporters contributed to an atmosphere reminiscent of a Chairman Mao or Kim Sung Il pep rally). At least 500 US 'fans' were in fact undercover agents (lounge-suited, sun-shaded, armed and speaking into wrist microphones – and therefore blending in perfectly). Hyped in the tabloids as Redskins versus Cowboys, highbrow broadsheets like *The Guardian* may well have been promoting it as 'Skin-Colour Genetically Dominant World Majority' versus 'Mutant Albino Genetic-Recessive Global Minority'[1] I preferred 'Sun People versus Ivy Leaguers'.

This home crowd differed from their co-hosts across the Yellow Sea by booing the opposition from the start, politely but passionately (which helped give the game some enthralling 'edge'). If Yokohama had felt like a pop concert, Daegu really seemed more like a political rally (democratic but full of registered party members).[2] For the American players it must have been a difficult, but by no means impossible, atmosphere to play in, being given the bird by fairly 'good-natured grunts' (to use ex-Vice President Dan Quayle's description of hecklers). They certainly didn't bottle it in the opening period, but tactically began by 'engaging the enemy on all sides' (in other words, getting themselves ambushed).

Brad Friedel in goal, however, played as if he had just watched John Wayne starring in *The Green Berets* to get himself pumped up. Red waves were threatening to engulf him – zoom football with go-faster stripes on – but he pulled off a series of fine saves. The Americans eventually managed to mount one dangerous counter-attack and New York Metro Stars' Clint Mathis deserves a soccer Purple Heart from his club when he gets home for his terrific strike in the 24th minute (even if his ghastly Mohican haircut made you want to turn away as he celebrated the opener, looking more like a World Wrestling Federation star than a pro footballer). The 60,000 South Koreans were stunned into silence. Then they started screaming like 30,000 stereos experiencing painful feedback.

Approaching half-time, Swiss referee Mr Meier awarded a soft penalty to the home team. The screaming was like high-pitched static on giant speakers, but it stopped dead when Lee Eul-Young's penalty was well saved by big Brad.

In the second half, it would have been a travesty if the South Koreans hadn't got something to show for all their attacking effort – zoom football with Warp Drive engaged – and they got an equaliser off the forehead of Ahn Jung-Hwan. The goal was good but the celebration was pure propaganda gold, as Ahn ran to the corner flag and proceeded to impersonate a speed-skater, one hand behind the small of his back, the opposite leg being lifted and flicked, and vice-versa. The crowd erupted in glee and joy, delighted that some Yankee noses were being put out of joint – especially those of the Winter Olympic judges who had disqualified Kim Dong-Sung at the Salt Lake City games earlier that year for the offence of 'cross-tracking', a dubious and controversial decision that had resulted in the gold medal being awarded to an American wimp and whiner called Appolo Ohno (unlike his honest, hardworking and honourable namesake Shingi Ono of Feyenoord and Japan). Hopefully this photogenic and televisual gesture made the American news headlines, in print and on television, because the US team were still struggling to get any coverage because of the ice-hockey Stanley Cup finals, for Chrissake.

With a minute left, penalty-misser Lee got to the by-line, hesitated fractionally and then pulled the ball back for unmarked Choi Yong-Soo. The goal was still wide open but the minimal delay in setting up the striker seemed to give him too much time to think. As the ball sailed harmlessly over the bar, Choi's heart must have sunk into his boots like an express elevator. Now there would be no life-size bronze statue of Choi Yong-Soo permanently on display outside the entrance to the Taegu Stadium (and in a way he must have been glad that he plays for JIF United in the Japanese J-League).

In their high-security compound the Yanks probably had to make do with telephone calls to their 'unpaid sex workers' – i.e. wives and girlfriends – but the South Koreans had earned a slap-up meal of scorched canine corpses and thru-the-night horizontal dancing in downtown Daegu.

In politically correct or culturally sensitive terminology, the score-line was probably honourable and for the best: South Korea 1, Turtle Island 1.

The Sun People had if anything too much ying, the Ivy Leaguers just enough yang.

NOTES

[1] Political correctness is easy to mock because it has gone too far, especially in America, but it was a genuine attempt to change language so that human beings weren't wounded by other human beings using terminology designed to denigrate or hurt.

[2] I was going to say the atmosphere was reminiscent of the Labour Party rally at Sheffield in 1992, but it wasn't complacently 'triumphant'. Can you imagine Guus Hiddink regaling his supporters with Neil Kinnock's excruciating: 'Are yer alright? Are yer alright? Are yer alright?'

31. Bend It Like Bouzaine

Tunisia 1 Belgium 1
Oita: Monday, 10 June, 10.00 a.m., BBC

Wilmots volleyed the Red Devils ahead in the first half but within minutes Slim Ben Achour had retaliated with a magnificent goal, which the Australian referee chalked off for a foul to *Tunisia*. From the free-kick however Rauof Bouzaine of Genoa curled in an unstoppable shot that Beckham or Carlos would have been proud of. And that was basically that.

At half-time, footage of the original speed-skating incident in Salt Lake had been dug out, but sadly the BBC didn't show the highlight of the whole Winter Games again – namely, the Aussie 'tortoise' who came from the back of the field to win gold as all the 'hares' in front of him collapsed on the final corner. Which could well have been a metaphor for the way this World Cup was unfolding, as favourites like France, Italy, Portugal and Argentina flirted with falling flat on their faces . . . As Gary Lineker admitted, 'I've given up making predictions.'

The second half was even less entertaining and Tunisia were no Algeria circa 1982, who I vividly remember beating what would have been the *West* Germans back then, 2–1 in Spain.

As this borefest limped towards lunchtime, I was reduced to trying to name Five Famous Belgians on a piece of paper. I was quite pleased with my list and thought it might win me a tenner in a pub bet one day (if I could remember it):

Paul de Man – disgraced deconstructionist writer and critic
Jan van Eyck – gloomy Flemish painter
Eddy Merckx – multiple winner of the Tour de France

Georges Simenon – sex-maniac novelist and creator of *Maigret*
Plastic Bertrand – 1970s one-hit-wonder pop singer

Five Famous Tunisians? Strewth . . . Five Famous Albanians would be easier to have a stab at: King Zog, President Enver Hoxha . . . and I give up.

Go on, you try it: name just one famous Tunisian. Carthage? That's a place, not a person.

Plastic Bertrand may be French not Belgian, but I'd give you very long odds against his being Tunisian by birth.

Hey, I've just remembered a sixth – Jean-Claude van Damme, the method actor and Shakespearean action-movie hero.

32. Two Jerzys Stretched in Jeonju

Portugal 4 Poland 0
Jeonju: Monday 10 June, 12.30 p.m., BBC

This match was, thankfully, the last of the second tranche of group games. Portugal restored some national pride and Poland added to their national embarrassment. The rainy season in this part of the world arrived after Pedro Pauleta's early strike and this sudden downpour seemed like Poland's last chance to turn the tide. But the rain was vertical and warm, not horizontal and freezing, and the pitch just slicked up instead of turning into a puddle quagmire. When Scottish referee Hugh Dallas ruled out an equaliser from Pawel Kryszalowicz, for an innocuous challenge on keeper Baia that a Scottish or Polish goalkeeper wouldn't even have bothered appealing about, the 'You're going home' writing was on the wall for Polish coach Jerzy Engel. The highly rated Liverpool goalie Jerzy Dudek was beaten three more times.

Two defeats and Poland were officially out, but Portugal lived to fight another day. Famous Pole Pope John Paul II played football as Karol Wojtyla and as Pope has created more saints than any of his predecessors, but neither of the two Jerzys mentioned above came anywhere near creating on-pitch miracles in Korea.

The final group games would kick off simultaneously, so that no two teams had the advantage of playing with knowledge of how their competitors in shared groups had fared earlier in the day, and I was looking forward to some exciting and dramatic finishes (and I certainly was not going to be disappointed).

33. Waterloo not Austerlitz

Denmark 2 France 0
Incheon: Tuesday, 11 June, 7.30 a.m., ITV

In the opening game against Senegal, David Trezeguet had smiled philosophically after hitting the woodwork at 0–0. At 2–0 down against Denmark, his smile was if anything broader after seeing his shot rebound off the underside of the crossbar. As confused admirers, supporters and backers of Les Bleus performed emergency post-mortems on the deceased French cockerel, which had strutted onto the pitch in Seoul just 12 days previously, I too wondered just how the World Champions had failed to progress (the first holders not to reach the second phase since Brazil in 1966). Trezeguet's *sang-froid* smirking in the face of unlucky adversity was perhaps a clue. His first flash of gleaming capped gnashers could be interpreted as psychological *savoir faire*, with the Juventus striker acknowledging both his remarkable skill and outrageous bad luck, remaining confident however that the first miss might conceivably cost him the coveted Golden Boot by a single goal but not thinking for a moment that it might cause his country to go down to defeat in their first fixture. The second wide grin was more problematic for a professional sportsman representing his country at the highest level, an indication that he had accepted the inevitable and that France were fated to lose and therefore exit the competition. In the highly charged circumstances, a more reasonable response would have been to grimace in psychological pain, raise eyes or fists to the heavens, spit in disgust or drop to his knees in despair. No one could accuse France of not trying really hard, of going through the defending-champion motions, least of all Trezeguet, but they definitely lacked the passion of the uncrowned, the hunger of the unsuccessful, and the determination of the unproven.

In 1998 France had won with the help of home support and not a little luck but without a recognised, never mind world-class, goal-scorer. In 2002 they had *two* (in Trezeguet and Henry) and even with the latter suspended for the Denmark decider they had two good strikers in reserve (Sylvian Wiltord of Arsenal and Djibril Cisse of Auxerre). Selecting Christophe Duggary of Bordeaux from the start instead of Cisse was undoubtedly an error, since this 30-year-old veteran plays like Chris 'Dug' Gary of Bathgate. A strapped-up Zidane appeared at last and with Vieira should have been able to take care of Toftig and Gravesen in midfield, but the bald mesomorphs resembling Phil and Grant Mitchell in *Eastenders* had as much trouble barring the French duo from the game as the Mitchells would have done turning Ian Beale and Arthur Fowler away from the entrance to the Queen Vic.

The failure of the French to score a single goal in the defence of their title will remain one of the abiding mysteries of this World Cup. The Senegalese had signalled a warning by ruffling more than a few feathers. The Uruguayans had brutally plucked some more. Denmark just throttled the big blue bird by its scrawny neck.

An escaped lunatic from a Parisian asylum had turned up in Incheon, dressed as Napoleon. A handwritten sign stuck in his hat read: '*On Veut Austerliz Pas Waterloo*'. At Austerlitz in 1805 Napoleon had defeated the combined forces of Alexander I of Russia and Francis II of Austria using battle tactics that still give military historians at Sandhurst and West Point wet daydreams. Roger Lemerre used to coach the French Army Team and was undoubtedly aware of the significance of the two battles. At Waterloo defeat was snatched from victory because of Napoleon's descent into conventional, safety-first tactics, with his 'lucky generals' convinced that they had only to turn up on the battlefield for victory to be assured.

As a secondary schoolboy playing organised, competitive war games, I owned my own set of elite French infantry – painstakingly hand-painted in authentic colours – and during one inter-school competition I was 'red carded' from the table because I refused our teacher's order to use my little models to charge British artillery units dug in on the crest of a hill. To have done so would have decimated my platoon and required me to prise my soldiers off their lollipop-stick bases, with five soldiers *glued* to each base (after the throwing of dice and measurements taken with a Perspex diamond to calculate casualties). I refused point blank, preferring to keep my pristine infantry marching up and down in reserve (or safe in their cotton-wool lined After Eight boxes).

Denmark deserved to win Group A and progress further because they wanted to win more than the French (and remember a reversed score-line would have seen France through to the second round). Even after Dennis Rommedahl fired the Danes ahead, three goals in reply would have done for France. But when Marcel Desailly hit the bar with his second-half header, you could see the fight visibly leaking out of the French. *Esprit de corps* collapsed and the Danes went in for the kill – Tomasson cleverly tugging Desailly's shirt before shooting home (which wasn't as unsporting as Desailly tugging Brian Nielsson's earlobe and giving it a sharp twist).

If pride goes before a fall, and the French felt like they were falling in a nightmare against Denmark, they definitely hit the ground before waking up in Incheon.

34. The Fat Man Resigns the Light Blues

Senegal 3 Uruguay 3
Suwon: Tuesday, 11 June, 7.30 a.m., ITV2

Uruguay may have reverted to cynical clogging type against the Fancy-Dan French, but in Suwon they mounted a glorious cavalry charge forward at three down and almost ensured qualification with a last-minute winner.

Feeling sorry for Uruguay was certainly a surprising feeling, but they got my sympathy vote as early as the 20th minute when Diouf sent himself crashing to the ground in the penalty box. In real time it looked like a stonewall penalty, but in replay and from a reverse angle Diouf obviously, but brilliantly, conned the referee. Khalilou Fadiga blasted past completely innocent keeper Carini. Senegal looked unstoppable and Uruguay certainly couldn't stop Diop adding two more before the interval.

Victor 'The Fat Man' Pua may walk the Sidney Greenstreet walk – i.e. waddle – but in the half-time team talk he talked the 'Ferrari'/*Casablanca* talk:

'How extravagant you are, throwing away goals like that. Some day they may be scarce . . . I came to Korea for the victories . . . I was misinformed . . . Abren, you're off; Morales you're on. Rick, I think this could be the beginning of a beautiful fightback . . .'

A mere 20 seconds in, Richard Morales scored, celebrating by removing his shirt (only to reveal an identical one underneath). Manchester United super-sub Diego Forlan volleyed a spectacular second. The Uruguay penalty was so soft it was positively Salvador Dalian in melting dubiety, with Dutch referee Wegereef possibly evening up the moral score after having seen Diof's blatant dive replayed on one of the big stadium screens. Recoba's left foot converted, with two minutes remaining. A winner for the South Americans in their famous light-blue jerseys and they would be through, at the expense of the Senegalese (who had been guilty of counting their chickens, all of them headless).

A Senegal defender headed a high-velocity shot off the line, from a height of 12 inches, and the ball spun straight up in the air. Rick Morales slightly mistimed his jump with the goal laid bare – and headed past the post with straining neck muscles bulging like the Incredible Hulk. Six inches to the left and it would have been Uruguayan ecstasy instead of Uruguayan agony. If only it had gone in for 4–3, Morales could have discarded two strips (assuming he had bulked up with three layers to celebrate a hoped-for hat-trick).

The Fat Man resigned as coach on the stroke of the final whistle. Sadly he wouldn't be celebrating in a Suwon nightclub with Dooley Wilson playing *Knock on Wood*.

'Play the video of the fightback again, Sam.'

'Yes, boss . . .'

This match was transmitted live on ITV digital, with the fightback goals shown during the Denmark–France game in split screen boxes. Surely, one of these simultaneously-timed matches could have been shown on ITV, with the BBC transmitting the other. This way terrestrial viewers could have channel hopped, or switched stations, or even set up a portable beside a regular TV. Of course, at 2–0 in the 'dead' Denmark–France game, ITV1 could have switched coverage to the exciting end of the Suwon game. By the time of the next World Cup, in Germany in 2006, I guess we'll all have digital services (although as I write today I do so without a computer, laptop, mobile phone, credit card, car, motorbike, mortgage, bicycle, central heating, double-glazing, contact lenses, video recorder, DVD, Gameboy or even a microwave).

So Senegal qualified behind Denmark, leaving Uruguay and France in their unexpected wake. My failure to put a fiver on Senegal at 250–1 was already causing me post-betting regret syndrome and heart palpitations. I would have to actively *unsupport* them from here on in.

35. Green Machine Negotiates Saudi Skid-pan

Saudi Arabia 0 Republic of Ireland 3
Yokohama: Tuesday, 11 June, 12.30 p.m., ITV

No matter the result in the Cameroon–Germany game, a two-goal margin of victory for the Irish would guarantee qualification. As the rain descended on a stadium full of green-clad fans, Mick McCarthy must have been reminded of Dublin's Lansdowne Road. Nasser Al-Johar, on the other hand, must have thought he'd died and not gone to heaven: 0–8, 0–1, a monsoon, 65,000 mad 'Irishanese' and 11 professionals from the English Premiership with at least one-seventh of Irishness in their genetic make-up.

One of the secrets of happiness was discernible in the relieved excitement and communal celebration which followed Robbie Keane's volleyed opener in the sixth minute – namely, to be part of a small group of like-minded human beings, working towards a shared goal (although I realise this definition could also be applied to the suicide-bombers of 11 September). By full-time, the 14 players who contributed to this win were probably the happiest 'Irishmen' on the planet; without doubt they were the happiest footballers who had won a football match played anywhere on earth on Tuesday, 11 June, 2002.

Other professions which supposedly meet Maslow's Hierarchy of Needs – from basic sustenance and shelter to swinging sex and self-actualisation – include hospital consultant, TV presenter, football coach, rock musician, opera singer, Formula One racing driver, airline pilot, independent publisher and film director. Even although auteurs of the cinema are often unemployed or resting, they are always negotiating deals or developing projects. When on set or location they are treated like creative kings, with an empire of fawning underlings who they can either use or abuse with their royal prerogative or turn into an alternative family or support group who are paid to supply unconditional love and respect and oral sex to a temporary but all powerful paterfamilias.

Most of us, however, get about as close to psychological self-actualisation in our dreary day jobs as we do to a bank vault full of gold bars with our names hallmarked into every piece of this precious metal. But the lucky few described above deserve their good fortune when they provide the rest of us with moments of sheer mental bliss, epiphanies of cerebral enjoyment when the grey static lifts and we feel glad to be alive (albeit experiencing life vicariously). Even supporters of Ireland during this match could be divided up in a hierarchy of pleasure obtained from the result. I know one old friend who was probably watching the match in a Dublin bar, surrounded by females, friends and family – an Irishman with a genuine love for football. His pleasure was undoubtedly greater than mine – watching it sober and alone and being only one-eighth Irish – but I still felt like I had ingested a capsule of time-released serotonin as the game went on. I'd rather have been one of the Irish players on the pitch, or an unused substitute, or member of the support staff, or one of the fans in the stadium, or a supporter supping a Guinness in a Donegal bar, but just watching on TV made me feel better and happier than I would have been viewing *Doctors* or *Neighbours* or re-runs of *ER* and *Ally McBeal*.

If Roy Keane was watching on TV, how must he have felt? As the Saudis came back from their bad start and began outplaying Ireland, was Keane totally indifferent or nervously worried or even secretly pleased and hoping for an equaliser? He may have the shoulder of Sir Alex Ferguson to lean on and the bosom of the Manchester United family to return to, but he must have been concerned about how rival fans would react to him in the new season. Maybe he would have to face four years of vilification *à la* Beckham. And would his largesse in admitting that he would be prepared to play for Glasgow Celtic when he could no longer hack it at Old Trafford still be acceptable to the Parkhead faithful (many of whom have historical and family links with the Republic)?

At half-time in the ITV studio, we were back in Des Lynam's 'Irish parlour' (into which trailers had been inviting viewers for days). As a pundit Andy Townsend was playing a blinder. As one of Jack

Charlton's 'plastic Paddies' he was never exactly international class on the pitch, but as a television pundit he was running rings round the other ITV panellists. Presentable, articulate, enthusiastic, amusing and perceptive, his confidence was growing with every live minute on air. Bobby Robson was little more than amiable, although referring to Ireland as 'we' was slightly confusing. However, since Ireland and England could only meet in the final, due to the seeding system and restricted draw, any switch back to 'they' was probably not going to be necessary.

Gary Breen scored Ireland's second in the 62nd minute and his broad grin seemed to vindicate his decision to turn down a new contract with Coventry City before departing for the Far East. As a free agent with a World Cup goal to his credit he had added thousands of pounds a *week* to whatever contract he eventually signed with whatever team. Damien Duff scored a third to put qualification beyond any doubt, although the juggling hash goalkeeper Al-Deayea made of dealing with the shot almost constituted an own goal (a sad irony since he had just become the world's most capped goalkeeper with 171 appearances).

Pleasing as Ireland's progress was to me personally, one statistical comparison with Scotland still made me wince. In three World Cups, the Republic had progressed out of the group stages three times. For Scotland the sad stats were, in American format, a dismal 8/0. An almost Saudi Arabian record of failure . . . It may not be easy being emerald green, but try being dark blue.

36. Chess with Violence . . .

Cameroon 0 Germany 2
Shizuoka: Tuesday, 11 June, 12.30 p.m., ITV

A 1–0 win for Ireland over Saudi Arabia and a 1–1 draw between Cameroon and Germany and lots would have been drawn to separate the Irish and the Cameroonians. But the Spanish referee in foggy Shizuoka was going for a world record and immortalisation in the *Guinness Book of Records*. At half-time, the score-line still read 0–0 but the game had already exploded into violent life. It was on a short fuse when Marc Vivien Foe pulled the shirt of one Torsten Frings. It went *kaboom* when Samual Eto'o was hacked down in a scoring position by Carsten Ramelow, who was sent off.

In the second half Germany may have been down to ten men, but Rudi Voller had at least hauled off Carsten Jancker for the more mobile Marco Bode, who scored a smart goal almost immediately. Klose then took his tournament tally to five in the 79th minute. Patrick Suffo collected a second yellow, like Ramelow, and also had to walk

Referee Antonio Nieto had booked seven players from each side, with an extra yellow for two on each side necessitating the two sendings off. A total of 16 yellows beat the previous World Cup record for a single match by *six* clear cards (held by Denmark and South Africa playing in 1998).

Völler complained afterwards: 'This isn't chess. It's the World Cup. There weren't any really brutal fouls.'

So Germany topped Group E with their usual magnanimity in victory and self-deprecating humour in a crisis. Ireland celebrated second-placed success, and Cameroon returned home in plaster casts for some intensive physical therapy. Saudi Arabia were just glad the whole nightmare was finally over.

At least Torsten Frings – the possessor of a truly great name – was still in the tournament and not suspended.

'Frings. Torsten Frings . . .'

'How do you do, Herr Frings. Pleased to meet you, I'm sure.'

'Similar feelings returned. Please call me Torsten.'

'Of course, Herr Frings. I'm sorry – Torsten. If you don't mind me saying, that's one cool name for a German dude . . .'

'*Ja*. Torsten Frings. I like it too myself. Have you met my international team-mate, Martin? Martin Max . . . Please explain inappropriate laughter in my face . . . From now off, Herr Frings to you!'

'Fuck you, Frings . . . Two fingers right back at ya, Torsten!'

37. Stomach-cutting Boredom in Osaka

Nigeria 0 England 0
Osaka: Wednesday, 12 June, 7.30 a.m., BBC

Playing for a draw which will take you through can be a very dangerous game – except when your demoralised opponents are giving reserves a run-out (including a teenaged goalkeeper). In order not to doze off, I pulled up the front of my England top and drew some cut-here perforation marks across my stomach with a green Stabilo Boss highlighter. Instead of a security blanket like Linus in *Charlie Brown*, I have a psycho-prop in the form of a brass scalpel with disposable stainless steel blades – but I had mislaid it somewhere. This left me struggling to maintain mental equanimity, since I've grown to depend on the reassuring feel of the cold handle and the frisson of quasi-sexual pleasure experienced when dragging the sharp tip down in between the tendons of my left wrist. I should perhaps reassure concerned readers that I'm not a suicidal personality; it's just comforting to know that the option is sitting there on the substitute's bench waiting to come on and end the whole stupid pointless game of existence called life. *Hara kiri* has no attraction for me personally, since you could still be conscious as your guts spilled out from your stomach. Similarly, decapitation would be a headless nightmare if consciousness wasn't obliterated the moment the spinal cord was split. Can you imagine the horror if you cut your head off, and then after watching your flailing limbs and torso keeling over decided to change your soon-to-be obliterated mind? *Brrrrr . . .*

The only highlight of the whole game was a Paul Scholes piledriver, which young Vincent Enyeama miraculously deflected onto the post. It was a spectacular and impressive save, but technically abysmal since he parried the Fevernova with the

133

incorrect hand, having reached across his flying body with his right arm instead of using the nearer left. Still, if he gets a transfer from Enyimba to one of the top clubs who employ his team-mates – such as Shakhtar Donetsk, Maccabi Haifa, Crewe Alexandra, Salonica or China's Gendi Boys – a professional goalkeeping coach would soon knock this showboating unorthodoxy out of him. David Seaman may have had a few backpasses to deal with, but frankly my attention was wandering. My cricket bat in close proximity calmed me down but where the hell was my scalpel? Christ, I couldn't very well go to meetings, or meet important people in trendy bars, with a cricket bat in tow, could I?

A 0–0 result meant Nigeria out, England through. Yawn . . . An immediate switch to the exciting conclusion of the Sweden–Argentina game woke me up and covered my arms in goosebumps (but that's for the next chapter). Two draws and a win from the 'Group of Death' was not bad going, but the sense of anti-climax was . . . like having had sex with a raddled heroin-addicted streetwalker in a seedy bedsit, as compared to having made passionate love to a power-dressed female executive who you've just picked up in a trendy cocktail bar before being dragged back to her minimalist penthouse apartment (I would imagine, in both cases). One goal from a corner and one from a penalty wasn't a record to worry Denmark, who England would now be playing in the cool of the evening. Victory over Nigeria would have entailed meeting Senegal in afternoon heat (but would have *avoided* an afternoon meeting with Brazil in the quarter-finals in favour of an evening kick-off against Japan or Turkey!).

Eriksson had been cornered by Garth Crooks in a corridor and the BBC's star interviewer told the England coach: 'Sven, I can confirm you have qualified.'

Sven looked disbelieving for a second, then, pounding a closed fist into an open palm, he shouted with emotion: 'Yes, yes, yes!'

Garth then delivered the bad news: 'Sven, I can also confirm you will be playing *Denmark* . . . but in the cool of the evening . . . not *Senegal* . . . in the blazing noon-day sun of a three-thirty kick-off . . .'

'Ah, that's a real disappointment . . .'

To be honest, only the first line of the above dialogue is true. It is however still unbelievable, since everyone had known for days that a draw would see England qualify. What Sven actually said was:

'No kidding, Gareth? Are you related to the Karlstad Crooks? Please keep taking your medication . . . or tell me something I don't know.'

If only . . .

38. Todo o Nada in the Group of Death

Sweden 1 Argentina 1
Miyagi: Wednesday, 12 June, 7.30 a.m., BBC Digital

Win, and Argentina qualified; lose and they went out. Hence their decision to play all-or-nothing attacking football. El Dorado or the *premio gordo* would require another four victories after escaping Group F, but if they failed to overcome Sweden the squad of the most highly valued players assembled for the tournament would be watching the final stages *en casa* (at home). Coach Marco Biesla had finally decided to play two up front, but once again Crespo was kept in heel-clicking reserve, with Claudio Lopez partnering Batistuta. Veron was dropped – after me giving him a eulogising chapter epigram! – in favour of Valencia's young Pablo Aimar. Previous coach Daniel Passarella couldn't have bettered the latter decision, for Aimar proved a midfield *supremo*, but disciplinarian Daniel would without doubt have marched every overpaid superstar down to the nearest *barbero* for compulsory short-back-and-sides. Most of the Argentine team resembled finalists in an Ozzy Osborne look-alike contest, detracting from the look of their all-blue, short-sleeved, '70s-style Adidas tops. The Swedes looked smart in their Adidas equivalents, but were playing in their traditional yellow.

Lopez immediately moved to the left-wing, but he and right-winger Zanetti were providing Batistuta with plenty of ammunition. With one Swedish prime minister gunned down in the recent past, Mjalby took this opportunity to throw himself around in front of metaphorical flying bullets like a Swedish secret-service operative determined not to lose another democratically elected head of government. He ended up taking some big hits but was obviously playing with a bullet-proof Kevlar vest attached to his strapping torso. The fact that he played the game of his life was reflected in the FIFA Man of the Match award. Keeper Hedman had few actual saves to make, but those that were necessary he pulled off brilliantly.

In first-half injury-time, the strain was getting to the Argentinian substitutes. Claudio Caniggia refused to stay seated in the technical area and referee Ali Bujsaim of the United Arab Emirates red-carded him for verbal abuse, by which time he had returned reluctantly to his seat. A baby-faced team-mate tried to take the rap in his place by starting to walk off, but ballsy Bujsaim was having none of it. He insisted that Caniggia take an early shower (using Timotei for his ridiculously long blond hair, no doubt).

At this level no team dominates for 90 minutes and Sweden earned a free-kick 25 yards out. It may have been a bit dubious but they deserved it after a miscarriage-of-justice booking for Larsson, who was punished for 'diving' after Gonzalez had physically assaulted him with extreme prejudice. Anders Svensson Beckhamised the ball and Sweden were one up.

At this point, in Buenos Aires a power-cut interrupted transmission of television pictures in some areas. The agony of Argentines gathered round transistor radios can only be imagined. Normal service was restored in time for the substitution of Batistuta, who at 33 and sporting long hair and a long beard walked to the touchline like Willem Dafoe in *The Last Temptation of Christ*. In the 88th minute Ortega sprawled hopefully to the ground in the box and fortuitously got the penalty. His kick was beaten out by Hedman, but with *four* Argentinians encroaching in the box before the kick was taken, there was little he could do about Crespo netting the rebound.

With four minutes left to play, this is where BBC 1 viewers got in on the action. I must admit I was willing Sweden to hold out, but wouldn't have been exactly dismayed to see Argentina pulling it out of the fire – because they had some of the tournament's most exciting players and unlike France had battled right to the end . . . But that day's script wasn't an extract from the middle pages of a *novella piccaresca* featuring Gabriel Batistuta as the romantic hero. At the full-time whistle, the big man was in tears, and for all I know the Argentinian *peso* collapsed on foreign exchange markets . . .

So the most unpredictable World Cup in history continued on its

Alice in Wonderland trajectory. Sweden topped the Group of Death, England secured their hoped-for second place, but *ahead* of Argentina, who said '*adios*' along with no-hopers Nigeria.

Hasta la vista, Argentina!

Or in the signing-off words of Gary Lineker: 'You can't win the World Cup today. Only lose it – just ask the Argentinians.'

39. Sun Sets on Rainbow Nation

South Africa 2 Spain 3
Daejon: Wednesday, 12 June, 12.30 p.m., ITV

This result would have had the Bafana Bafana dancing into the second-round phase, as long as Paraguay failed to beat Slovenia by 3–1 or more (and the petulant Paraguayans were soon to be a goal down and a man short). In the fourth minute, South African keeper Andre Arendse came off his line and went down in textbook fashion to smother an overhit through ball, but in his nervous excitement was flaffing at the Fevernova as if it had just come out of a hot oven. Raúl stuck a boot in between Arendse's flailing arms and then walked the ball into the net. As goalkeeping cock-ups go, it was an absolute howler, on a par with Al-Deayea's quasi o.g. against Ireland. Arendse must have played the remaining 86 minutes with a snake of anxiety gnawing at his intestines.

Benni McCarthy soon equalised, but a Mendieta free-kick on the cusp of half-time restored the Spanish lead.

South Africa fought back yet again, Lucas Radebe equalising with a fine header. But Raúl got his second and Spain's third in the 56th minute, although South Africa were still in a position to qualify as late as the 84th minute, when the unbelievable turn of events in Seogwipo meant they had to equalise to progress further. They tried their best but were obviously praying for a late goal by the Slovenians to help them out of Group B.

Bafana coach Jomo Somo was pacing his technical area liked a caged animal – and he must have felt like howling at the Korean moon rising over the Daejon Stadium . . .

40. Screaming Monkeys in Seogwipo

Slovenia 1 Paraguay 3
Seogwipo: Wednesday, 12 June, 12.30 p.m., ITV 2

With 65 minutes on the clock and ten-man Paraguay still trailing 1–0, coach Maldini introduced substitute Nelson Cuevas of River Plate to the action (which was about to heat up in quite hot-to-the-touch dramatic fashion). He dribbled past two static Slovenians and equalised with relative ease. In the 73rd minute fellow super-sub Jorge Campos of Catolica University fired in from 20 yards.

Under infamous President Stroessner, Paraguay had an international reputation for harbouring some highly dubious characters – from wanted war criminals to convicted drug barons – and the Slovenians reacted to the two substitutes as if Eugene Victor Tombs and Neetch Manley of *X-Files* infamy had just been thrown on with instructions to take people out (but not for dinner). The Slovenian defence began playing like a troop of screaming monkeys in a snake-pit. Nastja Ceh of Bruges came on to replace their goal-scorer Milenko Acimovic, but was red-carded within minutes of being given his big break on a world stage.

The resulting 35-yard free-kick was left to Chilavert to line up, and the goalkeeper with political ambitions must have been fantasising about how footage of the first keeper to score in a World Cup finals match might be edited for use in party political broadcasts. Only the fingertips of Mladen Dabanovic prevented Chilavert from declaring himself president for life at the post-match press conference, the Slovenian keeper managing to deflect the fast-travelling ball onto the crossbar, which reverberated as if it had just been clipped by the roof of an 18-wheeler truck passing underneath. Looking at his gloved hand with tears in his eyes, Dabanovic must have been wondering whether his fingers were broken or merely staved.

With six minutes remaining Cuevas collected the ball at the corner of the penalty box. He feinted right before cutting in-field and beating two defenders (who had at least forced him sideways). With a glimpse of goal and glory, he let fly with a blistering left-foot shot. The underside of the crossbar shuddered again but the ball still hit the back of the net. Cuevas celebrated like a man who knew he would never have to buy another glass of the narcotic national drink *mate* or a bottle of the popular tonic *yerba de urina*.

With neither South Africa nor Slovenia scoring in the next six minutes, Paraguay qualified second with one more goal scored separating them from the South Africans. Spain finished top with maximum points, having scored nine goals for the loss of four, while Slovenia were bottom with nul points.

41. Magic Realism in Sunny Suwon

Costa Rica 2 Brazil 5
Suwon: Thursday, 13 June, 7.30 a.m., BBC

As a guest lecturer at the Catennacio Bolt School of Soccer Coaching, located in the beautiful hills of Tuscany and subsidised by the Italian FA, Alan Hansen could show a full-length video re-run of this 'horror show' to highlight 'naïve defending' and 'diabolical positioning', but as a footballing spectacle this match was one of the most entertaining I have ever had the pleasure of sitting through (with more than a few interruptions for standing up and applauding). With Costa Rica playing the Beautiful Game like enthusiastic pupils and Brazil performing *futebol-art* like dancing masters, this was the football equivalent of literature's magic realism (as compared to the socialist realism inflicted on spectators by the likes of Russia and Poland). The only visual effect which jarred was Brazil turning out in white shorts, so as not to clash with their opponents' blue, and I had almost gotten aesthetically used to their Nike-designed yellow shirts.

The residents of Suwon who were lucky enough to get tickets would have felt no need for indulging in post-match cow-dung sniffing, a craze which the South Korean police had instructions to brutally stamp out.

With Brazil two up and with half-time approaching, a deflected corner from Junior fell far behind centre-half Edmilson, just below head height. Any attempted overhead scissor kick by your average centre-forward would have ended embarrassingly (and Emile Heskey attempting such a feat doesn't bear thinking about, frankly), but Edmilson caught it full and flush on the volley and thrashed it into the net for 3–0. (The last time I personally attempted a similar stunt, on the grass pitch in Millport on the Isle of Cumbrae,[1] I ended up on my arse after displacing a foot's worth of oxygen molecules in an air-kick that left me with a black-and-blue hip and a cricked neck).

In the second half Wanchope and Gomez got two goals back for their counter-attacking side and as things stood at this point, 2–3, Costa Rica would have qualified ahead of Turkey. Costa Rica continued to defend and attack, whereas Brazil were simply attacking and attacking. If one takes into account four rebounds from woodwork, some good saves and half-a-dozen other near things and missed chances, 7–10 would probably have been a fair reflection of the play. Brazil added two more to their actual tally, however, thanks to Rivaldo and Junior, goals which cruelly helped put plucky little Costa Rica out of the tournament.

Amazingly, Big Phil was not totally enamoured with his team's performance. His worry was that when faced with a strong, organised and disciplined defence, a stronger and better all-round team than Costa Rica might be capable of punishing carefree Brazil by soaking up the pressure and then exploiting the massive gaps left by Carlos and Cafu pushing up from their nominal full-back positions (often at the same time). Scoring at least one more goal than the opposition is of course the 'secret' of every winning team, but being prepared to lose three in the expectation of scoring four is a mindset that most modern coaches would pay sports psychologists to brainwash out of a squad rather than actively encourage. Defending your goal and keeping it intact is always easier and simpler than successfully attacking and penetrating an opponent's goal. One bad day at the office for the Brazilian front-line could conceivably see the whole team having to clear their desks and vacate the World Cup building.

Playing in such an attractive and life-affirming manner disguises the fact that for Brazilians the result is a deadly serious matter. When they lost the 1950 final 2–1 to Uruguay, in Rio's newly-built Maracana Stadium, the whole nation went into national mourning, to the extent that describing the loss as 'Brazil's Hiroshima' wasn't regarded as over-the-top hyperbole by the coiner of the phrase, Nelson Rodrigues. Like fans of literary magic realism, on the page rather than on the pitch, who erroneously assume that such works of delicious fantasy are not highly serious in political intent, admirers of the Brazilian attacking style should remember that the national team is *expected* to *win* (and with *style*). To win a World Cup is hard enough, but to do so while throwing defensive caution to the wind is a high-risk strategy requiring outstanding players and a fair share of luck. However, if Brazil were to go all the way to the final in Yokohama, every nation on earth – excepting that of their opponents on the final day – would be supporting them because of their style and attitude and Brazil are probably everyone's favourite second team (unless you're an Argentine, of course).

If this game had been repeated at night on say BBC Digital, and I had the service, I would cheerfully have sat through the enthralling 90 minutes all over again. Which is more than I can say for that classic of magical realist literature, *One Hundred Years of Solitude* by the Colombian Gabriel García Márquez (which, to be honest, I would need the title put into literal effect to ever finish reading).

Like Spain, then, Brazil topped their group with maximum points . . . with courageous Costa Rica ('the Wee Brazil') failing to get the second place their efforts in the above game deserved.

NOTES

[1] The town of Millport and island of Great Cumbrae don't feature much, if at all, in the books and few movies which have marked the recent 'cultural renaissance' in Scotland, which made the reference to them in the high-quality American TV drama *ER* all the more surprising and attention-arresting. Guest star Ewan McGregor's dying soliloquy in the arms of Nurse Hathaway, in which his fatally shot Scottish robber character extols the view of Wee Cumbrae from Millport as 'the most beautiful in the world' had this viewer laughing so hard I almost wet myself. The scene was played out dead-pan-straight by soon-to-be *Star Wars* superstar McGregor and lovely Julianna Margulies, and I'm surprised the tourist office on the promenade hasn't latched onto the marketing possibilities of the quote, with, say, a full-size cardboard cut-out of McGregor's Obi Wan with the deathless puff in tabloid-sized headlines underneath. It might not rival the George Sand blurb about Majorca being 'the most beautiful place that I have ever lived in and one of the most beautiful I have ever seen' but

it might pull in a few curious American tourists and Scottish *Star Wars* fanatics. Personally, I wish I could afford to visit Majorca every year, but Millport and Cumbrae will get my penurious custom until I die because they're actually pretty cool places in which to recharge frazzled urban sensibilities.

42. Turkey Shoot in Seoul Showdown

Turkey 3 China 0
Seoul: Thursday, 13 June, 7.30 a.m., BBC Digital

Missing live coverage of this match because of another simultaneous kick-off was no great sacrifice as a sports fan. Hasan Sas got the Turks up and running after six minutes, followed by Bulent Korkmaz four minutes later. It was Brazil's fourth goal in 63 minutes that actually did for Costa Rica and when they got a fifth a minute later Turkey knew that they could relax. Facing the Group C wooden spoon for accumulating no points and no goals, the Chinese began to take out their pent-up frustration on the Turks. Shao Jiaya made sure that even the FIFA Fair Play Award would be beyond their reach when he was red-carded for hacking down Belozoglu (our friend from the potentially explosive pushing incident in the Costa Rican technical area). Umit Davala made it three, three minutes from time. The Turks celebrated as if they had just won the World Cup, not merely qualified for the knock-out phase. (After eight anti-climactic attempts, if Scotland ever get through a group at a future World Cup, the players, supporters and fans back home are liable to party as if it's 2099. And if Scotland go out on goal difference in a group consisting of Afghanistan, Benin and Cape Verde in 2098 at least I won't be around to be 'cheerfully philosophical' about it.)

So Turkey sneaked second spot on a goal difference better by three than Costa Rica's. China coach Milutinovic quit, therefore avoiding having to explain the Great Footballing Leap Backwards to the mandarins of the Chinese FA . . .

43. Azzuri Prove Existence of God

Mexico 1 Italy 1
Oita: Thursday, 13 June, 12.30 p.m., BBC

God and justice are conspicuous by their absence in most human affairs, but this result proved their co-existence – at least to the satisfaction of Italian coach Trapattoni, who confessed to being a believer in his post-match press conference. Mexican coach Javier Aguirre[1] wasn't quoted in the British press, but a comment of 'We wuz bandido-ed' wouldn't have been unreasonable in the circumstances. (Thankfully Mexico is a Roman Catholic country like Italy, as are Croatia and Ecuador; otherwise such comments could be interpreted as pro-Catholic or pro-Christian, when, as every good atheist knows, the divine can be approached up the mountain of faith in any of three equally holy directions. Christianity, Judaism and Islam are three different routes to the godhead, routes which just happen to follow different paths until the summit is reached and God/Yahweh/Allah rewards climbers of whatever faith with eternal life and limitless contentment – or still doesn't show his face even when you've gone to the trouble of ceasing to exist in physical form just to spit in his eye.)

With Croatia expected to crush Ecuador in Yokohama, Italy had psyched themselves up for an essential victory over Mexico. John Motson mused mournfully that it would be 'interesting watching both games develop'. (Well, yes, John, but not all of us had BBC Digital services to exercise the option.)

At 33, Paolo Maldini was earning his 125th cap, but the AC Milan attacking left-back was approaching the age where a switch to central defence would have to compensate for declining pace and stamina. When his fellow defenders moved out en masse to catch Mexico offside, Maldini made the mistake of tracking back to mark Borgetti, who was chasing a high ball from Blanco. The Mexican out-jumped an out-of-position Maldini and with a twist of his powerful neck directed a reverse header past the stranded Buffon. The Italians had already seen an Inzhagi goal disallowed for offside and another strike was similarly disallowed later (both controversially, if you were Italian). But the Mexicans were in control and creating numerous half-chances.

Totti was yellow-carded for the newly defined offence of 'simulation' (i.e. diving or play-acting), which if prosecuted with the full force of refereeing law in Serie A next season is going to be like watching an opera without any singing, only the *recitativo*.

Still a goal down with five minutes to go, substitute Del Piero threw himself at an inviting hanging cross and glanced the ball past Perez. Motson confirmed that it was 'definitely not offside'.

For the four minutes of injury time, Mexico played the ball across their back four in desultory fashion, while the Italians remained furtively in their own half watching. The result from Yokohama had obviously filtered through, with Italy happy to settle for second place behind Mexico in Group G.

For the rest of the tournament, the Italian forwards would flirt with offside, carrying a great big chip on their shoulders. Maldini's fitness and form would be under continual scrutiny. Totti had earned himself a reputation for simulating. And the Italian public would be vocal in their demands for places to be found for Totti and Del Piero in the same starting line-up.

Italians, eh – what can you say? Well, most male Italians subscribe to the code of behaviour that requires a front of *machismo* to be presented to the world, in order to attract women who are attractive and well-dressed (the famous *bella figura* that Italian women pride themselves as having more of than other nationalities). At the same time, Italian males have no hesitation in living with their mothers until the day arrives when they finally take a bride. Bizarrely, Italy now has the lowest birth rate in Western Europe, which has less to do with declining sperm counts than a calculated desire for a higher standard of living and *la dolce vita*. As for supporting the national team, Italians as old as 19 genuinely feel incomplete as fans because they have not lived through the experience of the Azzuri winning a World Cup.

Driving in northern Italy, I was once flagged down by a police car. The officer who walked towards my driver's door was wearing designer shades and carrying a holstered pistol. He didn't speak English but my female passenger did (and her wealthy father owned the *gran turismo* two-seater). She did all the explaining and apologising, with tears of laughter rolling down her flushed olive cheeks. Apparently I'd been pulled over for driving dangerously *slowly* ('like an old grandmother going to Mass') and warned to pick up the driving pace in future. I was embarrassed and angry, but didn't quite have the balls to accelerate past the police Alfa-Romeo on a blind corner up ahead . . . Unlike Trapattoni I don't believe in God or justice . . .

NOTES

[1] Aguirre? Why does that surname ring a mental bell? I know: *Aguirre: Wrath of God*, Werner Herzog's weird 1972 movie about conquistadors under Pizarro floating down the Amazon on a raft. Klaus Kinski played Pizarro as clinically insane – i.e. without acting – and I remember watching it bored out my mind one wet Wednesday afternoon as an undergraduate. The college film club refused my repeated requests for Eric Rohmer's *oeuvre* to be shown in its entirety, dismissing his French films as 'boring and long-winded bourgeois drivel', so we got this German borefest instead. The sparse audience were all falling asleep until one of the Spanish soldiers took a long spear or arrow in the chest. Before keeling over into the drink, he declaimed: 'Hmm . . . long pieces of killing wood are back in fashion, I see' (or words to that effect). We all laughed hysterically, not because it was funny as such but because it was such an incongruous and unexpected line for such a tediously melodramatic art-house clunker. Our laughter had a hysterical edge, because we were very bored and extremely unhappy, suffering from Glasgow College of Technology Cabin Fever. I like my art-house cinema to be set in France, Spain or Italy – and in the 20th or 21st centuries. Anything set before I was born struggles to get my attention and the more contemporary a movie's place in history the more likely I am to sit through it. For instance, no matter how brilliant the film was, I don't think I could endure a film set in 17th-century Finland, with a female central character in her 80s as the heroine. I need to watch stuff I can relate to personally – which is why female narrators of novels have me dozing off in my armchair. I don't mind female leads in

149

movies, especially if they're Nastassia Kinski or Demi Moore or Greta Scacchi getting their kit off and making love to the camera. And as Dennis Pennis memorably asked Ms Moore: 'If the integrity of the script demanded it, would you keep your clothes on?'

44. Croatia Crash to Earthquake Experts

Ecuador 1 Croatia 0
Yokohama: Thursday, 13 June, 12.30 p.m., BBC Digital

A win would have got Croatia through, but 'creative differences' were rumoured to be spreading through their camp like a dose of clap in a co-ed dormitory. The heroes of France '98, Davor Sukor and Robert Prosinecki, were banished to the bench, where they sat sulking like passed-over Oscar nominees. Alan Boskic came close to scoring twice, but only Robert Redford-look-alike Robert Jarni was trying his utmost and playing well. These 30-something stars had ended up in some strange places in the twilight of their careers. Jarni was probably happy with the pay and conditions at Panathinaikos in Greece,[1] but Sukor had ended up at 1860 Munich, Boksic at Middlesbrough and poor old chain-smoking Prosinecki was 'unattached' to any club, unless you counted a somewhat tenuous connection to Portsmouth.[2]

With Croatia appearing as if they didn't give a damn, but getting angrier and angrier at their failure to get anywhere, Ecuador's Edison Mendez celebrated his neat 48th-minute finish by extending his arms like an aeroplane and running half the length of the pitch. I was chuffed for him, because although he plays for Deportivo, it's the Ecuadorean club Quito not the Spanish La Liga outfit La Corunna. With Italy equalising late on, a Croatian goalbound header cleared off the line in injury time wouldn't have made any difference anyway.

Ecuador still finished bottom, but at least they went out on a high. Most of their squad would be returning to earthquake-prone Ecuador but five of their number had pre-season training with Barcelona to look forward to, Delgado a return to sunny Southampton and good old boy Ulises de la Cruz the prospect of promenading up and down those great European thoroughfares Easter Road and Leith Walk.[3]

NOTES

[1] I was once invited to start a new life in Greece but turned down the kind invitation. Otherwise I could have been watching World Cup 2002 and writing this book in a summer house in the Peloponnese.

[2] I also once turned down a good bourgeois job in Portsmouth of all places, which if I'd accepted it could have seen me living today in a suburb of Pompey with a saloon car, a wife and 2.4 children. Phew, lucky escape.

[3] As it is, I normally walk down Easter Road and up Leith Walk about once a week – and each time I battle through wind and rain to get the deposit money back on glass bottles of Irn Bru, I'm confirmed in the rightness of past decisions. Especially when I've had a drink in every pub en route.

45. The Triumphal March Continues

Tunisia 0 Japan 2
Osaka: Friday, 14 June, 7.30 a.m., BBC

A dreadful first half resembled football *pachinko* (pinball), but only a Japanese crowd would have broken into song with Verdi's *Triumphal March*. Half-time reading matter was probably equally unique, with manga magazines being flicked through by everyone from schoolchildren to grandparents (these comic-book publications feature the kind of graphic sex and gratuitous violence that Channel 5 would be prosecuted for broadcasting in real-life format). I half-expected Troussier to be handing out *hachimaki*[1] at half time, since these headbands are worn to indicate that the wearers are trying to get some serious work done (as well as keeping the sweat out of their eyes). Students wear them when demonstrations are intended to become riots, as well as donning them for important examinations. Kamikaze pilots tied *hachimaki* round their heads, and I'm sure if the Japanese team had reappeared wearing them, the Osaka supporters would have exploded with appreciation. In the first half the team had played as if kitted out in *geta*, the traditional wooden clogs with an inherent design flaw – namely, a strap for the big and second toes situated in the centre of the clog (and which inflicts on the wearer a knock-kneed gait). For the record, Tunisia couldn't have played any worse if they'd been wearing flip-flops.

In the dressing room, Troussier may have sat down cross-legged for a quick Japanese tea ceremony, but if he did the volatile Frenchman must have succumbed to the urge to throw some crockery around *à la* Alex Ferguson. It would be interesting to know if Troussier's ever-present translator converted *everything* from French into Japanese, including any expletives, or if he applied linguistic emollients. Indeed, if Group H rivals Russia had any Moscow Mafiosi in the Nagai Stadium, they could have made the translator an offer he couldn't have refused: to contradict in Japanese everything Troussier said in French.

Within minutes of the restart, home-town substitute Hiroaki Morishima had used his lack of height to nip in and score. With the pressure off, along with the substituted Inamoto, Nakata was centre-stage and responded to the squeals of delight whenever he touched the ball by running the midfield single-handedly. He wrapped up the game with a fine diving header, ensuring not only qualification for his country but top place in the group for Japan.

NOTES

[1] These headbands or headkerchiefs can be miniature versions of the *nisshoki*, or national flag, depicting the rising sun as a red ball against a white background. The version so beloved by graphic designers is actually the imperial navy flag, with red rays emanating from the large red spot.

46. Last Call for Aeroflot Tokyo–Vladivostok

Belgium 3 Russia 2
Shizuoka: Friday, 14 June, 7.30 a.m., BBC Digital

A draw would have been enough for the Russians, while nothing short of victory would suffice for the Belgians. One of the Russians, of course, began by hacking down a Belgian in a dangerous free-kick position. Johan Walem lined up his kick like a rugby full-back, before floating the ball away from a standing-to-attention Nigmatullin. Members of the ramshackle wall began to get their recriminations against their keeper in early, before he could explode at them.

Apparently the Russians were on much larger financial bonuses than the Belgians – for each stage of progression in the tournament and for winning the World Cup – but any direct correlation between monetary reward and improved performance is hardly hard and fast. Would China have fared any better if they had been on a million pounds a man to reach the second round? They would simply have collected more yellow and red cards and committed many more fouls.

Romantsev's team-talk must have involved talking softly but carrying a big stick, because his downhearted charges put up a bit of a fight in the second half. Miss-of-the-tournament-man Beschastnykh managed to score, after having missed another sitter, and Russia were beginning to grind the Belgians down. Robert Waseige took coaching action by introducing the *enfant terrible* of Racing Genk, Wesley Sohk (and I hope I'm not transposing names here). He out-jumped ten Russians and their goalie from a corner, heading in and celebrating with a somersault. Waseige, who looks like Mr Shorofsky the music professor from *Fame*, may have sneaked a smirk at Romantsev but he himself was caught on camera taking a comb from his blazer pocket and running it through his silvery mane, patting down his hair to his vain satisfaction with his free hand and looking smug and self-satisfied. When Wilmots made it 3–1, I half expected Waseige to break out the Cossack hairspray. Dmitri Sychev got one back to make it 3–2 and the Russians finally began to bombard De Vlieger in the Belgian goal. Twice the camera cut to Waseige on the touchline, who wasn't exactly pulling his hair out but who was exhibiting the kind of physical nervousness not to be recommended for an overweight 60-something who has already undergone heart surgery.

Soon after the final whistle, Romantsev resigned. Victor Onopko, the captain winning his 100th cap, was quoted as saying: 'I would like to apologise to the people of Russia. This loss was a tragedy.'

At least this Russian defeat led to no reported deaths in the Motherland.

47. 'My Name is Sanchez. Angel Sanchez . . . OFF!'

Portugal 0 South Korea 1
Incheon: Friday, 14 June, 12.30 p.m., ITV

A draw would have seen both teams qualify from Group D – assuming the USA lost to Poland – and although the Portuguese would have been cynical enough to play one out for 90 excruciating and embarrassing minutes, the South Korean supporters would never have forgiven their team if they had indulged in such negative match-fixing. Instead of reciprocating any sly nod-and-wink attempt to reach an 'understanding', the South Koreans went for the Portuguese jugular – and the Portuguese didn't take kindly to such honest aggression. Joao Pinto's brutal tackle from behind on Park Ji-Sung could reasonably have been interpreted as having leg-breaking intent. Angel Sanchez of Argentina had no option but to red card Pinto, who reacted like the aggrieved party. His team-mates lost any semblance of self-control, especially captain Fernando Couto who repeatedly cupped the referee's frightened face in his hands. A summary dismissal for Couto should have followed, but maybe Sanchez was justifiably worried about having his nose broken by Couto's forehead.

In the second half, Portuguese tempers had subsided somewhat but they rose on the psychological Richter scale to psychotic red when Roberto Beto collected a second yellow and was dismissed. Lee Young-Po of the Anyang Cheetahs certainly went down like a gazelle being caught by the fastest animal on the planet, even if replays suggested he made a meal of the tackle and was guilty of a degree of 'simulation'. Four minutes after the second sending-off, South Korea scored through Pinto's genuine victim of assault, Ji-Sung chesting the ball under control brilliantly, flicking it up and past Sergio Conceicao and whacking it past Baia with his left foot. With less than 20 minutes left,

Guus Hiddink must have felt like Ernest Hemingway having downed a charging elephant, with one more strike necessary to put the animal out of its misery. Portugal, however, down to nine men, had other ideas and they began to play their best football of the tournament, wounded but highly dangerous. South Korea had further chances to kill the game, but not as many opportunities as a desperate Portugal had to equalise. As time ticked by, the tension level was increasing in unbearable increments. With two minutes left, Conceicao rattled the inside of a post and with the last kick of the game forced Lee Woon-Jae into making a fine save.

A draw would have saved the 'golden generation' of Portugal players from a humiliating exit, as well as kept South Korea at the top of Group D (which makes the co-host's decision to go for a win all the more admirable). Portuguese coach Anton Oliveira left his technical area on crutches. A broken leg soon knits together, but a broken heart can hurt more and take longer to heal.

48. Punch-drunk Yanks Win on Points

Poland 3 USA 1
Daejon: Friday, 14 June, 12.30 p.m., ITV 2

With the pressure off, Poland let rip, going two up in the first five minutes against an American team that had finally descended back to their 'natural' level. Poland hit the woodwork and had a penalty saved by Brad Friedel before adding a third in the second half. Landon Donovan's consolation goal near the end was largely irrelevant, since the USA owed their second-placed progress to South Korea's winner against Portugal.

With all the qualifying groups completed, Portugal joined France and Argentina as pre-tournament favourites who had fallen at the first hurdle. Watching minnows rattling a few cages is always fun, but when the cage-door is shoogled open and colourful parakeets released to a fate of being pecked to death by grey sparrows, it's not a pretty sight (*I know, I know – this mixed metaphor is clunky and almost meaningless, but as a reader you'll know what I'm trying to say*). Would Senegal, for example, provide more viewing pleasure than displaced France? Would Sweden be more fun to watch than Argentina? Would the USA be able to match the potential on-field fireworks that Portugal would have been expected to contribute?

Back in the ITV studio, after highlights of Poland–USA, Des Lynam was stitched up by his production team in a tedious look-alikes feature. A line drawing of Mark Twain was flashed up on screen, and I suppose there was a passing resemblance, what with the grey hair, grey moustache and spectacles. Given the almost dream-like unbelievability of the shock results that had been registered so far, with giant-killing worthy of a football fairy tale, I'll wrap up this section of the book – with the knockout second-round matches about to kick-off – with a quote from Mark Twain:

When I'm playful I use the meridians and parallels of latitude for a seine [net], and drag the Atlantic Ocean for whales! I scratch my head with the lightning and purr myself to sleep with the thunder!

For whales captured in daydreaming reveries, read France, Argentina and Portugal . . . *Folie de grandeur, Française! Hasta la vista, Argentina! Saudade, Portuguesa!*[1]

NOTES
[1] Basically, 'Yearn your heart out, Portugal.'

49. Oliver's One-man Army

Match One: On the Friday night I made sure my radio alarm-clock was set for 7 a.m. and rummaged through the bathroom medicine cabinet looking for Nurofen Plus painkillers. Frustratingly I had run out, which in my case is a bit like an asthmatic mislaying an inhaler or a diabetic running out of insulin. An incipient migraine would have to be knocked on the head, so to speak, with a good night's sleep (which I clearly recall having had many, many times in childhood).

My dreams don't need any fancy Freudian interpretations to figure out any subconscious significance – I dream about what I consciously worry about, albeit in Dali-esque surroundings – and as I tossed and turned I imagined I had a metal plate in my head, which I feared was about to set off security alarms as I queued anxiously for an airport metal-detecting machine. All hell broke loose as I walked through and the flashing lights and screaming sirens had me on my knees holding my throbbing head in an attempt to stop it exploding . . .

I awoke to the sound of the radio blaring away and I staggered across the room to thump the snooze button (the greatest invention of the 20th century). The pain behind my right eye was just about bearable and I tried to make it disappear with valium, paracetamol, aspirin, Dif 118s, coffee and Lucozade – plus some solid food (*yuk*) – lest it developed into a full-on, debilitating migraine attack.

One giant that hadn't been killed off in the culling fields of the qualifying groups was, of course, Germany, a country and team whose greatest strengths and worst weaknesses are probably efficiency and obedience. Their ability to churn out results in football competitions is unique, comparable to their economic miracle since the Second World War. Given a logistical objective and reasonable resources, the methodical and problem-solving technocrats on the football pitch or in the company boardroom will find the most cost-effective solution to achieving measurable success. Even when winning three World Cups, and losing in three finals, no neutral would have paid good money for the aesthetic pleasure of watching them in automated action, but they play the game of football to win – and do so with monotonous, and in some ways, admirable regularity.

Although Czech, Franz Kafka wrote in German and if he had not died of tuberculosis in a Viennese sanatorium in 1924 he would probably have shared the fate of his three younger sisters, all of whom perished in Nazi concentration camps. *The Trial* and *The Castle* can be read as foreshadowing the horrors of the Holocaust, but maybe Kafka would have lived to see America, having written *Amerika* without even having visited the country. Another of my favourite writers, Walter Benjamin, committed suicide while trying to escape to America in the late summer of 1940, the 48-year-old German-Jewish liberal intellectual being refused entry to Spain by obdurate border guards the day before killing himself. Modern German sensibilities are scrupulously sensitive about this dark part of their history and of course those born after 1945 have nothing to feel personally guilty about.

(My publisher says I could be the next Franz Kafka or Marcel Proust, which is very flattering except for the fact that I hate Proust and find him unreadable.)

Only 25,000 fans turned out to see the first second-round knock-out match between Germany and Paraguay, leaving the 42,000-capacity Cheju Stadium bereft of any atmosphere. I naïvely hoped that Paraguay would once again 'go for it' as they had done in such exhilarating fashion against Slovenia, but they seemed content to try and play out a 0–0 draw. The bloody Germans played for a functional 1–0 win, and eventually achieved it, even though they had to wait until the 88th minute.

Bayer Leverkusen's Bernd Schneider burst down the right wing like a holidaying Bavarian with a towel sprinting to claim a poolside lilo. He crossed for club colleague Oliver Neuville to volley past furiously-mad Chilavert. Watching Neuville play for Leverkusen in the Champions' League run, all the way to the final at Hampden, I'd assumed that he was *French*.[1]

So 1–0 to Germany, then, and they were in the quarter finals – again.

My notes on this game started off illegible and soon became non-existent. The pain behind my right eye had intensified and spread. Feeling nauseous, I wrapped some frozen peas in a towel and retired to bed with a plastic basin. I switched on the portable black-and-white TV at the foot of my bed and awaited the England game and the vomiting – and the only question was which would start first.[2]

NOTES

[1] France may have been out of the official World Cup, but they won the first prisoners' World Cup. The infamous Bangkok Hilton in Thailand had allowed jailbirds from eight countries to compete, on a makeshift pitch within the confines of the barbed-wire prison walls. Most of the players were serving time for drug-running. The French foreign nationals won, on penalties. Any would be author on the winning side could easily get a publishing deal as the 'new Henri Charriere', author of the best-selling *Papillion*, but whether French coach Roger Lemerre could be persuaded to write the introduction would be another matter.

[2] In his book *Migraine*, Oliver Sachs suggests that migraine attacks could be nature's way of making neurotics lie down for some much-needed bed rest Hmm . . . From painful personal experience, I have found that being laid up for up to 48 hours in a darkened room is anything but restful or recuperative. Propping oneself up on one elbow to retch up bile every 30 seconds or so, while enduring a headache that can only be described as thermo-nuclear in intensity, is an experience I wouldn't wish on my worst enemy (or rather I would, especially if it relieved my suffering instantaneously at the same time). I've had classical migraines all my admittedly neurotic life and the only silver lining is the six hours or so after an attack has subsided. The sense of relief and normality is such that I feel I could conquer the world. In recent years, however, I've developed 'basilar migraines', which include all the usual symptoms but with the addition of paralysis and blindness! At its worst I resemble a blind quadriplegic who has overdosed on emetics. But migraine

is a sign of creative genius and fellow sufferers have included Sigmund Freud, Leo Tolstoy, Frederic Chopin and Virginia Woolf (who first developed migraines after she caught her brother looking up her skirt – and he, not surprisingly, never recovered from the shock either).

50. Elsinore Castle Collapses

Denmark 0 England 3
Niigata: Saturday, 15 June, 12.30 p.m., BBC and ITV

Match Two: The tabloid trials and tribulations of Beckham and Eriksson were put into trivial perspective when a Danish magazine ran a story about Stig Tofting on the eve of the Denmark–Uruguay game. *Se Og Hoer* revealed that, as a 13-year-old boy, Tofting had returned home from school to find that his father had murdered his mother, before turning the murder weapon – a gun – on himself. Although the decision to run the story, and at such a sensitive time, was universally condemned in Denmark – with many newsagents refusing to sell the issue – the revelation dominated the Danish media for days. His unofficial adoption by a local chapter of the Hell's Angels gave the story another macabre twist. At 32, however, 'Lawnmower Man' had succeeded in piecing his life back together at Bolton Wanderers and proudly bore a tattoo on his barrel chest which read: 'No regrets'.

Eriksson may have been embarrassed at having his alleged affair with Ulrika splashed all over the red tops, but his long-term partner Nancy Dell'Olio was in the Big Swan Stadium to give her man moral support and sexual relief. Danish coach Morten Olsen had lost his young wife many years previously, when she disappeared over the side of a ferry-boat travelling between Denmark and Germany. A presumed suicide, her body was never recovered.

As a fan, one of the attractions of competitive football is actively supporting your team, to the point where you are so engrossed in the action that everyday worries and recurring negative thoughts disappear for up to 90 carefree, glorious minutes. As a professional player engaged in the physical action, or as an ambitious coach concentrating on analysing the play, personal concerns must be pushed even further back from conscious attention. One can't help but wonder if at any point during this match, especially when it was as good as over, if Tofting or Olsen allowed their thoughts and memories to dwell on these personal tragedies. Human consciousness is both a blessing and a curse, a 24/7 operation which can literally drive sentient life forms round the psychiatric bend. A healthy mind must operate like a sharp stylus on a well-cared-for vinyl LP, but a crazy person must feel as if the needle is sticking and/or jumping across scratched plastic grooves in the consciousness of their troubled minds. *Don't think about it* is of course an injunction that the disturbed human mind feels compelled to ignore: *except all the time, every minute of every single waking hour until the blessed relief of drink/drugs/death blots everything out.*

BBC and ITV were sharing coverage of this game and I'd decided to opt for the former when the latter trailered their programming with Lynam boasting of ga-ga Gazza: 'Choose the man who shed a tear. He is one of you.'

'He's not one of me, mate,' I felt like screaming at my TV. Apparently Gazza 'corpsed' at least once and never managed to complete a sentence without getting embarrassingly tongue-tied. Over at the BBC, Dane Peter Schmeichel's use of English and acute observations not only put Gazza to shame but Peter Reid as well (whose speechlessness may partly be explained by the fact that his club's goalkeeper's market value was plummeting with every attempted save).

At kick-off my head was still pounding, but at least my stomach contents had remained undisturbed. The Danish defence looked as if they were playing with bad hangovers, Martin Laursen in particular seeming to be in the grip of *delirium tremens*. A highly rated Serie A centre-half with AC Milan, he headed a harmlessly bouncing high ball out for an unnecessary corner as if pink elephants were floating across his field of vision. From Beckham's corner, Ferdinand rose at the back post to head the ball straight back across goal. Sunderland's Thomas Sorenson reacted like an alcoholic with the early morning shakes, down on his knees, fluffing at the ball as if it were a feral pussy-cat. He only succeeded in scooping the ball over the line (although the goal was later officially awarded to Ferdinand as a fifth-minute opener). I rose like Dracula from his coffin to cheer the goal and almost passed out from the pain set off inside my skull.

Michael Owen got off the mark with a fine left-foot finish and 'dangerous' Denmark were turning out to be as intimidating as a collection of crash-test dummies. Ebbie Sand came to life once but he shot wide when he should have scored. After more *Keystone Cop* defending 1–2 soon became 0–3, when a Mills throw-in rebounded from the back of Nic Jensen's head and Beckham squared to Heskey, whose skidding long-range shot in the rain slithered under a shell-shocked Sorenson. Game over and England were in the quarter finals.

At half time I started throwing up violently and switched over to ITV for the aural entertainment value. Clive Tyldsley was just as competent as John Motson behind a microphone and without Motsy's irritating obsession with what we Brits were eating and drinking as we watched. 'Every time you see him [Tofting], you can't help thinking he threw you out of a nightclub at some point . . . You wouldn't try to beat the door policy again, would you?' Nice one, Clive. Now if only you could combine commentating with translating Big Ron into English. 'We're all going to be in the Big Yo' turned out to be a chicken-counting reference to Yokohama, venue of the final.

England benefited from a Danish defence which was about as decisive as Hamlet, and an opposing goalkeeper auditioning for the role of Ophelia, but if you come up against under-performing opponents determined to lose, all you can do is accept Yorick's skull, put it on the mantelpiece and move on to the next battle.

51. Golden Goal Taken by Camara

Sweden 1 Senegal 2
Oita: Sunday, 16 June, 7.30 a.m., ITV

Match Three: After a first-half headed opener by Larsson and a deserved equaliser from Camara, this match went into Golden Goal extra time. FIFA are reportedly having second thoughts about this innovation, since its introduction and the prospect of one goal ending a match in peremptory fashion has resulted in ultra-defensive play during periods of extra-time. Previously a lost goal was a serious blow, but it still left that most motivating of factors: hope. Even if an equaliser failed to be conjured out of the remaining minutes, the losing team still had the opportunity to get themselves out of trouble and an incentive to throw caution overboard during an exciting finale. With Golden Goals, the losing team is left feeling utterly deflated, and although such goals are decisive they leave an unpleasant feeling of anti-climax at the end of such games. Personally, I've never felt comfortable with the rule, smacking as it does of artificial Americanisation. Statistically, it makes penalty shoot-outs less prevalent, but penalty shoot-outs are exciting and dramatic (as well as being a test of nerve and skill under intense pressure, with a lottery element that just adds to the televised human theatre).

Even in intense heat, Sweden and Senegal both went for the knockout goal. Without any fiver riding on the Africans, I was rooting passionately for the Scandinavians. John Champion was providing an informative and amusing commentary, which is more than can be said for ex-England boss Graham Taylor's match analyses. Champion cheerfully and cheekily reminded Taylor that 'tomorrow would be the tenth anniversary of Sweden's 2–1 win over England in Euro '92'. Taylor huffed and puffed in phoney self-deprecation at the unwelcome reminder. Sadly he didn't reply: 'Do I not like that!'

After 112 minutes of strength-sapping and nerve-wracking football, Anders Svensson almost became world famous in Southampton, Sweden, Scandinavia, Europe and the whole football-watching world. Nicknamed the Cannonball Kid after his free-kick against Argentina, he revealed some subtler but even more breathtaking weapons in his attacking armoury. Larsson headed the ball to his feet and facing away from goal, two dragbacks with the studs of both boots on the surface of the Fevernova left Ferdinand Coly stranded in his wake. Svensson quickly composed himself and hit a right-foot shot destined to bulge the net. It rebounded off the outside of the post and a pivotal moment had come and gone. The boyishly handsome 25-year-old held his face as crushing disappointment threatened to overwhelm his fine features.

Two minutes later Camara was running threateningly at the heart of the Swedish defence. Inside the penalty area before he could be professionally fouled, his left-foot shot was slightly sclaffed but deadly accurate. The Fevernova tumbled agonisingly towards Magnus Hedman's far post, where it deflected into the net for a Golden Goal that turned Dakar into the party capital of Africa. In Stockholm, Swedish fans must have deflated faster than a barrage balloon riddled with bullets from the first synchronised propeller and machine gun.[1]

The Swedish players looked physically exhausted and psychologically shattered, while the Senegalese, led by Diouf, celebrated by line dancing in front of each stand. Camara was carried high on the shoulders of team-mates as the hero of the hour, a turnaround in fortune that must have been difficult for this 25-year-old soccer journeyman to get his head around. Coach Metsu had unceremoniously dropped him from the squad after an inept performance in the African Nations Cup final, where Camara missed two open goals, and his peripatetic club career had involved a going-nowhere sideways progression from Zurich Grasshoppers to Xamax Neuchâtel to Sedan of France. His World Cup displays had put him in the shop window equivalent of Harrods and his football career credit rating had suddenly become AAA platinum. Larsson, on the other hand, was so devastated that he announced his retirement from international football in the Swedish dressing room, shaking hands with his tearful team-mates after having scored 24 goals in 72 appearances for Sweden.

It may have been a Golden Goal for Senegal, but it was a lead balloon in the groin if you were Swedish (and the extreme emotions would have been exactly reversed if Svensson had scored instead of hitting the post). If extra-time had continued for another six minutes, Sweden could have equalised or even won the match. And if they hadn't done either, they would have had 360 seconds to reflect on an increasingly likely exit. For neutral fans, an additional six minutes of viewing pleasure was arbitrarily denied. On reflection, I reckon the Golden Goal is gratuitously cruel and skews the structural framework of matches into misshapen sudden-death cul-de-sacs.

Being an ITV game, we went straight to commercials, where I sat slack-jawed at the ad for the new Vectra. It starred respected character actor and B-list Hollywood star Ed Harris, playing a motor executive trying to appreciate the advanced aesthetics of this new model. 'What's so prestigious about pristine blue?' he philistinely enquires. His starring role in a British car commercial surprised me, since he had just been promoting his recently-released movie *Pollock*, a labour of love apparently, which he directed and starred in as the eponymous painter. Jackson Pollock was a drunken depressive, whose drip paintings brought him fame and fortune as the leading figure in the abstract expressionist movement. His 'action painting' was supposed to 'offend' the political left, the political right and the middle classes (although how splodges of paint on canvases which depicted nothing recognisable in lived existence could offend anyone politically is beyond me). However, his 'subversive' paintings and self-destructive personality were assimilated into the political and artistic mainstream. This 'success' was a failure that did Pollock's none-too-stable head in. And Harris had made much of the challenge of bringing such difficult material to the screen, since it was deemed uncommercial by most studios. And here he was flogging a car in a phenomenally well-paid commercial, with the advertising slogan, 'New Vectra, New Rules.'

For Chrissake, Pollock was killed in a car crash!

NOTES

[1] As inventions go, succeeding in synchronising the rhythm of a machine gun with the number of revolutions per minute of a propeller may not be up there with discovering penicillin, as far as helping the human race to live better and

longer goes, but it still amazes me to think that a pilot can squeeze the trigger of a machine gun mounted directly behind a propeller and not shoot the revolving blades to smithereens. I just don't understand how it is possible. Just like I'll never understand how the earth's orbit round the sun, which I know takes 365 days, somehow means that the northern hemisphere of our planet has approximately six months of summer while the southern has six months of winter (and vice versa). I've had it explained to me twice, once with diagrams, but I still don't *understand* it . . . I am however a literary genius, not a scientific wonk . . .

52. Tilting at Windmills

Spain 1 Republic of Ireland 1
Suwon: Sunday, 16 June, 12.30 p.m., BBC and ITV

Match Four: When Fernando Morientes headed Spain in front in the eighth minute, the writing appeared to be on the wall for the Republic. With Raúl in constant danger of escaping Ireland's offside trap, only the margin of Spanish victory seemed in question. But with their backs to the proverbial wall, the Irish lads hung on for dear green life and gradually fought their way back into the contest. The dribbling of Duff in the second half was hypnotising the Spanish defence to the point where their facial expressions of disgust resembled audience members selected by a stage mesmerist and persuaded to believe that the apples they were eating were really onions. In the 62nd minute Duff won a dubious penalty, exhibiting skilful simulation, but my heart sank when the taker turned out to be Ian Harte. His form so far had been poor and he didn't look like a man who was relishing the opportunity to wipe the slate clean (at the risk of accumulating yet another black mark against his name). His penalty was under-hit, too straight and the perfect height for Casillas to parry. Kevin Kilbane had no doubt been encroaching but his headstart to reach the rebound almost got him on top of the ball too quickly. Nevertheless, he should have been able to tap-volley the ball into the unprotected net; instead he went for blootered glory and ended up slicing the ball horrendously wide with his left foot.

A less committed team than Ireland would have let their heads drop, even playing out the remaining half hour on their knees, but like Dostoevski – who wrote his greatest books after being blindfolded and made to face a firing squad (with a last-gasp reprieve saving him) – Ireland just kept plugging away. Spanish coach Camacho shot himself in the foot, twice, in a fug of tactical panic. Morientes and Raúl were, inexplicably, both substituted, lessening the likelihood of a killer goal on the break (and leaving Spain toothless in attack if the match should go into extra time). With big Quinn on, and heartbroken Harte off, Ireland once again threw coaching-manual caution to the wind. The Spanish defenders weren't just rattled, they were shaking with trepidation. Quinn in particular was a Don Quixote figure, turning central-defensive Spanish knights into flailing windmills. With a minute to go, captain Fernando Hierro was pushing and pulling the back of Quinn's shirt up towards the striker's shoulders, like a sex-mad homosexual in a prison rape scene directed by Pedro Almodóvar. The nearest thing the World Cup had to a refereeing sex symbol, Anders Frisk of Sweden, bravely but correctly awarded Ireland a second penalty. Sly shirt-tugging in penalty-box mêlées is socially acceptable in professional circles, but Hierro's moment of shirt-ripping madness was inexplicable. Human beings, eh? There's no telling what they'll do under pressure.

The penalty still had to be converted. Robbie Keane buried it like a hardened gravedigger. 1–1. Like Lazarus, Ireland were back from the dead once more. Harte hugged Keano like Mrs Lazarus.

In extra time emotions were obviously running high on the Irish bench, but if there is one reasonable criticism that can be made of Mick McCarthy and his managerial team, it's that no-one was professional or level-headed enough to spot that Spain were reduced to playing the entire 30 minutes with only ten men. Having used all three substitutes, an injury to David Albelda meant that he could not be replaced (and in the heat of battle no one even noticed). Tactically this could have made a big difference to Ireland and the information would have lifted Irish spirits on the park. (Personally, I wouldn't be too critical, because as a football-match reporter in a previous life, I phoned in incorrect score-lines, completely missed substitutions, misidentified scorers and once even forgot which way two competing teams were supposed to be playing – and who they were.)

Much scientific research has been carried out into the art or science of penalty-kick taking, and one oft-quoted finding that seems to make subjective sense is that in a five-kick shoot-out, the penalties should be taken in reverse order of ability, so that the best players are left to convert the decisive, high-pressure kicks at the end. Ireland, on the other hand, let Keane get them off to a scoring start. Hierro, who must have been feeling guilty as sin and nervous as hell, coolly converted his side's first spot-kick: 1–1.

Matt Holland's run-up was strangely truncated and in a last-second attempt to generate extra power he lifted the ball over, clipping the crossbar. Ruben Baraja then sent Shay Given the wrong way: 1–2.

David Connolly shot softly and straight at stationary Casillas. Juanfran Garcia went for the right corner but side-footed past the post: 1–2.

Kilbane, after his sliced sitter of a miss, at least hit the target, but Casillas guessed right and easily palmed away the shot. Juan Carlos Valeron looked confident and must have thought he'd scored when he first hit the Fevernova – but it hooked like a golf ball and struck the left-hand post on the way past: 1–2.

Steve Finnan went high and left, leaving Casillas helpless: 2–2.

Gaizka Mendieta looked like he was lining up to give evidence to the Spanish Inquisition. Replacing the ball on the spot after initial misgivings is never a good sign. Either Mendieta was psychologically suffering, fit to burst into tears, or he was a head-game merchant playing a game of double-bluff with Given. His kick turned out to be the effort of a scared man with rubber legs and lead boots. The ball *trundled* towards the centre of the goal, like a rabbit's mis-hit golf drive, but Given had already initiated a dive to his right and his trailing boot couldn't quite reach the ball: 2–3 to Spain on penalties.

In such situations, players are remembered not for scoring but for missing, but a missed penalty isn't a moral crime. It may constitute a failure of nerve, or mental weakness under psychological pressure, or just plain bad thermodynamic luck, but it should not be regarded as a stain on a player's character. If Holland, Connolly or Kilbane had tried some training-ground trickery and failed to pull it off – like lining up to hit with a right foot and then using the right leg as a pivot for a left foot swinging around from behind to hit the ball with an instep – then they could have been condemned. Otherwise, there were no villains, only heroes.

Strangely, the player I felt most sorry for was Shay Given. The young Irish keeper had been interviewed in the build-up about his memories of Italia '90, when Packy Bonner had saved from Daniel Timofte's spot-kick to put Ireland into the quarter-finals. Young Shay had headed for his back garden, where he pretended to be his hero Bonner, for hour after hour. Twelve years later, through no fault of his own, Given had failed to save a single penalty. The Mendieta scuff must have been hard to take, another example in football of a shot being so unexpectedly bad that its very incompetence makes it virtually unstoppable.

I felt disappointed but not deeply so. After the Roy Keane fiasco, Ireland could easily have ended up performing like Saudi Arabia, Tunisia, France(!), Slovenia, China or Nigeria. They had instead played some quality football, provided air-punching last-minute excitement and added to the gaiety of watching nations with some good craic and endearing human-interest stories. Quinn had been the last to leave the pitch at Suwon, having played his last ever game for his country, and he certainly had some good stories to tell any grandchildren sitting on his knee in the future. Mick McCarthy had secured his job and possibly the keys to the city of Dublin.

Back in the ITV studio, Bobby Robson had been elevated to 'Sir Bobby Robson' in the Queen's Jubilee Honours list (along with 'Sir Mick Jagger'). I must confess I groaned in despair at the thought of another clutch of titles and baubles being handed out to the great and the good. I know I'm never going to be offered one, but in the unlikely event I would undoubtedly tell them where to shove it. I mean, knighthoods for establishment figures and MBEs for lollipop men and dinner ladies. Doesn't anyone turn down these tawdry trinkets?

Yes, apparently, because later in the evening I watched Jon Snow presenting a Channel 4 programme called *Secrets of the Honours System*. Newscaster Snow has in the past turned down an OBE, because it would have compromised his journalistic integrity, and although they wouldn't speak to him on camera it was interesting to learn that Sir Trevor McDonald, Sir David Frost, John Simpson (CBE) and Kate Adie (OBE) had all seen fit to accept such grace-and-favour patronage.

I hope the Republic of Ireland honour their players and manager with a heroes' welcome, but not with phoney letters before or after their names.

53. A Noodle Western

Mexico 0 USA 2
Jeonju: Monday, 17 June, 7.30 a.m., BBC

Match Five: This bruising encounter brought together, for the first time, two teams whose countries shared a geographical border – one side of which is known as the servants' entrance to the USA. It is one of the longest land borders in the world – and the outright busiest. Ironically, the US government spends millions of dollars trying to keep out the 'wet-backs' from Mexico, even though the economy of Los Angeles and Southern California depends on cheap Latin labour to keep it booming. Another historical irony is that if not for the Mexican Wars, Southern California, Arizona, New Mexico and large parts of Texas would today be run from Mexico City.

Mexico were desperate to win this fixture against the gringo college boys from the Land of the Free. Imagine a football-mad Scotland playing an England team of Oxbridge 'amateurs', because an alternative-reality England only really played rugby, cricket, hockey and netball as professional sports. This was a footballing *High Noon*, but remade as a noodle Western by Sergio Leone. Instead of the respective national anthems, an Ennio Morricone soundtrack blasted from the Jeonju Stadium loudspeakers. The hand-held Arriflex camera panned down the team line-ups, with the Americans dressed in ponchos and chewing cigarillos. The unshaven and rank Mexicans were wearing sombreros and staring into the camera with dead eyes, snarling psychotically . . .

Eight minutes in and Claudio Reyna broke down the right, cut the ball back to Josh Wolf, who flicked it into the path of unmarked Brian McBride. He cocked a muscular leg and bulleted the ball past Perez into the net. Whereupon the Americans reconstructed the Alamo in their own penalty area. Like Santa Anna waving his 4,000 troops forward, coach Aguirre indicated for all his outfield players to pile forward. An American handball went undetected, but not by the Mexicans. Tempers were beginning to boil blood in throbbing veins.

With 15 minutes left, Fulham reserve Eddie Lewis crossed for Donovan to make the game safe – statistically and results-wise, but not physically if you were an American. With seconds remaining Mexico captain Rafael Marquez managed to both head-butt substitute Cobi Jones and kung-fu kick him in the stomach. It merited two red cards and criminal prosecution rather than the single red he got. If perpetrated on legendary Jim Bowie, the culprit would have been carried off with the famous knife between his shoulder blades.

For such an attractive fixture, or potentially explosive one, the stadium was disappointingly half empty. As co-commentator Joe Royle pointed out: 'The fans keep trying to start a Mexican Wave, but it keeps falling down the holes in the ground.'

Interviewed by a US network reporter, coach Arena said: 'Our guys left their being on the field today.' A bit like the Alamo, then – except that America won and were in the quarter-finals.

Clint Eastwood came to prominence in the US public consciousness in *A Fistful of Dollars*, playing the man with no name. Despite a phone call from President Bush congratulating the American team for their victory by 'two touchdowns to nil' most Americans were still ignoring their soccer squad's marvellous achievements, only vaguely aware of the team's existence, and in affluent households across the US there were few who could name any member of the squad.[1]

In Mexico, however, effigies of the starting 11 were burnt as part of the festival called *The Day of the Dead*. New heroes to rival Pancho Villa and Emilio Zapata had failed to materialise and all Mexico was in mourning.

NOTES

[1] The unfairness of this result did bother me. The USA were rampaging through the tournament, but not disturbing a sea of indifference amongst sports fans back home. A Mexican victory would have made millions and millions of poor Mexicans ecstatically happy for a few memorable hours and

boosted national self-esteem dramatically in the long-term. Americans are bloody lucky to live in America but if anything they are too rich and comfortable for their own good. For example, compare and contrast the following two publications: *Caledonia* and *W*. The former magazine is a Scottish lifestyle magazine, glossy but thin (physically and editorially). I got a free copy with a recent edition of the *Daily Mail* (which I only buy on a Saturday for its brilliant seven-day TV supplement). *Caledonia* must struggle for enough 'exclusive' advertisers and 'up-market' readers. The June 2002 edition had an excruciatingly naff feature called 'Tips from the Top', where 'people at the top in business, politics and the arts' were pumped for pithy tips on what it takes to be a success. For example, Bill Campbell of Mainstream Publishing, was quoted as saying: 'Success is being far too busy to compose an amusing anecdote for this feature.' Is it really? Should have asked me, because I've got a lot of free time and am good at composing amusing anecdotes. Honestly, this magazine is fit only for toilet reading and arse-wiping.

On the other hand, *W* magazine is an American lifestyle magazine, the glossy pages of which run to 536. It is 95% advertising, from companies like Prada, Ralph Lauren and Dolce & Gabbana. It positively reeks of conspicuous consumption and serious money and is designed to be languidly flicked through while weekending at the Hamptons, I would imagine. In one way it is a disgusting publication, but it is also a successful work of art in and of itself. This is the American Dream on glossy paper and I treasure my March 2001 edition. Such opulent lifestyles may not make anyone happy, but it sure beats buying supermarket own-brand baked beans to make ends meet. If I ever set foot in America, I'm never coming back (unless it's in a box or shackled at the ankles with an expired visa in the breast pocket of my boiler suit).

54. Belgium Bounce Off Big Coconuts

Brazil 2 Belgium 0
Kobe. Monday, 17 June, 12.30 p.m., ITV

Match Six: With the Brazilian carnival on the move from Korea to Japan, the prospect of having the background noise of Samba rhythms and Bossa Nova bands interrupted by Ron Atkinson was too much to bear. I turned the TV volume down and turned on Radio Five Live. Commentator Alan Green would have been informative and entertaining, but his commentary was driving me crazy within minutes. The wireless descriptions of the on-pitch action were of course more detailed than Clive Tyldsley's television equivalents, but the radio broadcast was almost two seconds *ahead* of my television pictures. Ninety minutes of this and I would undoubtedly have been sectioned under the Mental Health Act of 1988 – for exhibiting all the symptoms of paranoid schizophrenia ('Honestly, Doc, my hearing is out of synch with my vision'). So it was back to Clive and Big Ron (making about as much sense as a stroke victim self-medicating with tabs of acid).

Plucky little Belgium were giving hip-swingingly arrogant Brazil a master class in organisation and commitment. Brazilian goalkeepers are normally as highly rated as Scottish tennis players, but Marcos was proving to be confident and competent. The Jamaican referee Peter Prendergast was subjected to much post-match criticism for being neither, but the main point of controversy in the game was actually a decision he got absolutely *right*. Jacky Peters had pumped a long ball upfield, where captain Marc Wilmots rose superbly above Roque Junior to head home what looked like a deserved and indisputable opener. But extended full-length replays showed that just as Peters released the cross, Wilmots had punch-pushed his marker in the small

179

of the back, just enough to unbalance Junior when he tried to jump with Wilmots. The fact that Wilmots didn't complain at the time said a lot (although he did afterwards), but a critical mass had been reached amongst pundits determined to heap opprobrium on officials from wee diddy countries. The Wilmots leap and header was constantly replayed at half-time, from various angles and close up, but his illegal nudge had been committed seconds earlier. It was, however, a let-off for Brazil and Big Phil must have been bursting blood vessels at half time, trying to convince his players to follow a conventional game plan. One can imagine Cafu and Carlos sitting nodding and smiling in theoretical agreement, before going back out and completely ignoring managerial instructions.

If Wilmots had had the pace of Michael Owen, Brazil would have been out. But with the Three Hip-Swinging Rs on the park – Rivaldo, Ronaldo and Ronaldhino – Belgium were sweating buckets and almost asking for a cold shower. It arrived in the 67th minute, with Rivaldo doing some ball-juggling with his back to goal. Suddenly he was facing the right way and letting fly with his flashing left foot. A cruel but possibly academic deflection saw the Fevernova whooshing past underemployed De Vlieger. Rivaldo celebrated like Harry Belafonte in a yellow simmet vest, waving his shirt like a lassoo.

Belgium's last chance for glory fell to Mbo Mpenza in the 72nd minute, the star of Excelsior Mouscron with a reputation for crashing Porsches and Ferraris into stationary objects. He blasted wildly over the bar.

Ronaldo shot through the Belgian keeper's legs before the end, when Belgium were wagering the equivalent of house deeds on throwing a seven or eleven at a crap table.

Belgium had been bloody good throughout the game, but Brazil had been brilliant once – when it really mattered – setting up a quarter-final against England. Knowing the Belgians, recriminations and imprecations in French and Flemish probably filled their dressing room. Belgium's frustration was understandable, because against themselves and Turkey, Brazil had been there for the knocking over, like a great big coconut on a sideshow shy. But had Big Phil actually succeeded in sticking a spot of glue to the base?

55. Time to Hit the Drinking Shops and Love Hotels

Japan 0 Turkey 1
Miyagi: Tuesday, 18 June, 7.30 a.m., ITV

Match Seven: The penultimate second-round match gave 'Team Japan' the opportunity to apply some psychological pressure on their fellow overachieving co-hosts 'Corea'[1] – and on paper Turkey were not as stiff a test as Italy. Both Japan and South Korea had pulled off PR coups in their staging of the tournament, combining efficient organisation and warm hospitality. Blue replica team shirts were just as numerous and noticeable in Tokyo as their red equivalents in Seoul (although bizarrely the Japanese capital was not selected as a venue, its denizens having to make do with the 'suburb' sites of Yokohama and Saitama). The 5,000 or so riot police waiting in strategic side streets beside stadiums had mercifully not been called into action, with visiting fans simply enjoying the football and the cultural experience. Apart from a few bad decisions by referees and linesmen, the World Cup 2002 was progressing like a well-oiled dream-machine.

Philippe Troussier had begun his campaign with a popularity level on a par with General McArthur accepting the Japanese surrender, but group qualification had seen his approval rating approaching that of the Emperor (who had to sign a bit of paper after the Second World War stating that he was no longer a god). As one of the twilight army of mercenary managers who tout their coaching CVs around various football associations, Troussier had once found himself accepting employment by the Burkino Faso FA. A modern-day Joseph Conrad or Graham Greene could well find inspiration in these coaching itinerants for novelistic anti-heroes. Troussier earned himself the sobriquet *Le Sorcier Blanc* (the White Witch Doctor) and executive-class accommodation in the capital Bujumbura. The success he was finally enjoying with Team Japan would make a dramatic difference to future employment prospects, and he could have been forgiven for harbouring daydreams about updating his CV by pressing the print button on a laser printer to add: 'Friday, 31 May–Sunday, 30 June, coached Japan to victory in World Cup 2002'. Even without leading his inexperienced squad all the way, he had done enough to expect a pencilled-in appearance on short-lists for all of football's top jobs – maybe even for his home country, where Roger Lemerre was not exactly being talked up by peers for a Legion of Honour award.

By kick-off Japan's rainy season, the *tsnyu*, had well and truly arrived. Stewards had handed out complimentary pac-a-mac ponchos to the 50,000 fans, whose enthusiasm remained undampened. 'Nippon! Nippon! Nippon!' they chanted in high-pitched unison.

An early corner for Turkey should have been a formality to defend against but the Mohican-anonymous Davala rose unmarked to head into the far corner. Tsuneyasu Miyamoto, in a Lone Ranger mask worn to protect a facial injury, had completely lost the late-arriving Davala. Replays from behind the goal identified a surprising culprit in the form of Shinji Ono, who was in position beside the far post when the corner was taken but who inexplicably moved sideways *away* from the goal when the ball was in the air. If he'd stayed put in textbook manner, remaining where he should have been, the goalbound header could well have been headed clear.

Turkey spent the rest of the game refusing to look this gift horse in the mouth (whatever that means – something to do with unexamined teeth?). Just before half time Brazilian-born 'Alex' lined up a free-kick for Japan, and his shot cannoned back off the junction of post and crossbar. His reward for coming so close was to be substituted at half-time, along with goal-threat Inamoto. Troussier's tactical thinking seemed to be bending under the pressure and goal-scoring hero Morishima wasn't introduced until the final five minutes. Troussier attempted to explain himself by citing strategic necessity. 'I needed players on the bench capable of winning the match in extra-time.' Hmm, Philippe . . . The obvious retort is that you can't hope to win in extra-time if you can't extend the game that far. The zoom football of previous games had ground to a disappointing halt in the downpour and Japan exited the competition like a damp squib. A stunned silence greeted the final whistle, with more than a few tears shed amongst players and supporters. Troussier had not proved to be the 'second shogun' or his players genuine soccer samurai. The lap of honour, in the driving rain, could have been directed by Kurosawa (who could never have enough movie rain in *The Seven Samurai*). But the crowd eventually overcame their crushing disappointment and managed some polite clapping.

Still, things could have turned out a lot worse for Team Japan, who actually failed to win a game during the finals of France '98. Any such repeat performance on home soil would have condemned the players to the social level of the *burakumin*, social outcasts in Japanese culture whose ancestors carried out the dirty work of the economy (such as removing sewage or slaughtering animals). They still account for one in fifty of the population and are prevented from being assimilated into the mainstream by thorough checks on family bloodlines before marriage – which if, for example, applied to people of Afro-American descent in America would quite rightly provoke international outrage.

Japan, however, had done well enough on the pitch to infiltrate football into the consciousness of the Japanese public. Unlike in the USA in 1994, where the World Cup came and went without turning Americans on to soccer as another national sport, enough seeds of passionate interest had been sown on newly-fertile ground to expect a future harvest of football-mad Japanese supporters. Japanese culture might even adapt to the concept of outstanding individuals who can show society new ways of doing things. This tournament may have ended disappointingly for the fair-weather home fans – but, hey, that's the natural condition of being a football fan: eternal disappointment. But as Confucius might say, 'It's the journey what counts, mate, not the arrival or destination' (unless you're lucky enough to be German or Brazilian).

NOTES

[1] The appearance of scarves in South Korea with 'Corea' emblazoned across them was an understandable two-fingered gesture to their co-hosts. During the Japanese occupation, the invaders had insisted on the 'K' spelling of the country, because it came after 'J' in the alphabet.

56. There's Only One Guus Hiddink

South Korea 2 Italy 1
Daejon: Tuesday, 18 June, 12.30 p.m., BBC

Match Eight: In 1966, Pak Doo-ik became the pin-up boy of the North Korean communist way of life, a sort of footballing Che Guevara, when he scored the goal that eliminated Italy from the World Cup. The North Koreans may then have succumbed to Portugal in the quarter-finals 3–5 (after leading 3–0 at half-time) but nobody north or south of the DMZ expected South Korea to emulate their achievement. Nevertheless, match commentary was blasted across the artificial but heavily fortified border.

I was struggling during the initial minutes to decide who was going to have my support. A fifth-minute penalty award for South Korea still had me swaying on my psychological fence. Italy were cool as hell but South Korea were hot, hot, hot. A penalty concentrates the mind of any watching neutral and I knew I would soon find out who I was subconsciously favouring by my physical reaction to the outcome of the kick . . .

'Bugger!' I bellowed, holding my head in instantaneous despair as Buffon parried Ahn Jung-Hwan's shot. The fringe player with Perugia in Serie A had scored only once for his Italian employers all season – and with finishing as bad as this it wasn't a surprising statistic. But the miss prompted me into the South Korean camp, so that when Vieiri scored from a corner soon after, I slumped back into my armchair. Like Japan, South Korea had revealed an Achilles' heel that was likely to prevent them progressing any further: an inability to defend corners. Vieiri had been man-marked, and shirt-pulled, but he's built like a bull and his strength at the near post made him unstoppable.

'*Daehan min gouk!*' chanted the 40,000 fans, meaning 'We must win!' Like the Turks against Japan, Italy set about killing the game and silencing the fans. But the South Koreans in the stands simply wouldn't shut up and the Red Devils on the pitch refused to stop running. If the Italians hoped that the South Koreans would eventually wind down like clockwork toy soldiers, they were sadly mistaken; if anything they were still going like Duracell bunnies as the clock ran down towards the 90th minute.

Commentator Barry Davies observed: 'Trapattoni didn't get where he is today by playing attacking football.' Defending against Oriental dervishes still takes its physical toll and Christian Pannucci's legs were beginning to buckle at right-back. With two minutes left, he intercepted a pass in the middle of the box, but instead of clearing decisively he well-nigh collapsed on the spot. It bounced off his exhausted body, which resembled a *Thunderbird* puppet with its strings suddenly cut, into the path of Seol Ki-Hyeon who swivelled with superhuman strength and blootered the ball past Buffon. In the dying seconds, Vieiri missed the sitter of his life – sliding in beneath the crossbar to somehow send the Fevernova high and wide (which at least cheered up Russia's Vladimir Beschastnykh, who was no longer in the running for the Concrete Overcoat for worst miss of the tournament).

Plan A hadn't worked for the Italians but Plan B at least involved trying to score a Golden Goal. Totti found himself bearing down on goal, and half of Italy must have been on their feet in front of their TV screens. But midfielder Song Chong-Gug had chased him all the way back and managed to get a foot to the ball before making bruising contact with the Italian star. If the ball hadn't been flicked away, Totti could probably have retained his balance to score; instead he went down like a murdered lover in an Italian opera. In fairness, he may have found it difficult to remain standing, but he milked his fall for a hoped-for penalty. Common-sense refereeing would have 'punished' him by turning down the appeal but Mr Morena of Ecuador went for the option of a second yellow card for simulation – and Totti was off.

In the second period of extra-time, Damiano Tommasi thought he had beaten the offside ploy and had the ball in the net. But once again the linesman had his flag up. Replays showed it was a very marginal decision, if not downright wrong. The modern interpretation of the offside law is supposed to favour strikers when there is any doubt, but Italy were on the receiving end of yet another 'misinterpretation'. Their predicament merited some sympathy but instead of rolling their sleeves up and getting on with it, they began to wallow in hysterical self-pity. Trapattoni was pictured looking at a small monitor on a desk and then thumping the plexiglass wall between him and a FIFA official. The whole team seemed to be composing conspiracy-theory excuses in their heads, while the Red Devils just kept coming at them from over the horizon.

With three minutes left to reach the lottery of penalty kicks, South Korea went instead for the glory of the Golden Goal. The ball was swung into the box and penalty-misser Ahn Jung-Hwan rose majestically in front of a rooted-to-the-ground Maldini. His flicked header found the corner of the net and it was all over. The Italians dropped to their knees while the South Koreans celebrated like UB40 card-holders whose six numbers had just come up on the televised Lottery show.

For South Korea, a nation that hadn't won a World Cup game in 14 attempts before this competition, the degree of success being achieved was approaching the religiously sublime. Amazingly, they had beaten three Roman Catholic teams in the shape of Poland, Portugal and Italy. And their quarter-final opponents would be Spain.

The Italian response was a sad reflection on a great sporting nation. Okay, the bad luck they had to ride in this game was the equivalent of a bucking bronco, but what were South Korea supposed to do, apologise for winning? The Italian FIFA delegate Rafael Ranucci claimed South Korea were a powerful country and that 'it was clear they had done something'. The referee was described as 'something you would only see in a comedy film'. Perugia promptly announced they would not be renewing Ahn Jung-Hwan's contract. RAI, the Italian state broadcaster, threatened legal action against FIFA, for loss of anticipated advertising revenues. Well, at least the *finita la commedia* (the game is over), the Red Devils could have retorted. They played football using *accelerando* – an Italian musical term for gradually increasing speed – until their opponents' heads were spinning.

A massive banner proclaimed: 'Guus Hiddink for President'. Hiddink smiled benignly and serenely as his players linked hands in a line and ran into both penalty areas, before diving in synchronised fashion along the grass. I couldn't help but compare this with the funereal walk-round the Japanese players had been forced to complete.

The Seoul businessman with the contract for producing Guus Hiddink dolls must have been rubbing his hands with glee. The so-called 'Irish of Asia' had put one over on their co-hosts and I was delighted. Millions took to the streets to celebrate, but disappeared at the stroke of midnight with their rubbish bagged and binned.

Hiddink had found the culture shock of his new job somewhat difficult to cope with, but hopefully he found time for a late-night celebratory meal, downing champagne, OB beer and yet more *kimchi* (the staple diet of South Koreans, a hot peppery sauerkraut concotion that plays havoc with Western digestive systems).

Barry Davies deserves the last word here, despite an excruciating attempt to speak Korean at extended length at one point. With regard to the Italians, he lost any BBC neutrality when he concluded: 'They lost it because they will not *learn*.' Meaning sitting on a lead instead of extending it. They may have been technically superior but they didn't have hearts as big as their heads.

'Guus Hidd-inki, un *tahk hana-da*!'

Exactly.

57. Start Crying Your Heart Out

England 1 Brazil 2
Shizuoka: Friday, 21 June, 7.30 a.m., BBC and ITV

Match A: The organising committee had managed a seamless transition from the group stage to the second round, with football being played on 14 and 15 of June without any frustrating hiatus in the never-ending on-screen action. Progressing from the second round to the first of the quarter-finals, however, necessitated a two-day break without any live football. With only eight games left to be played, I was already dreading the end of the tournament. After the final on 30 June, there was nothing to look forward to! By the time of the next World Cup in Germany in 2006, I would either be dead – or forty-fucking-five years fucking old! Wimbledon 2002 would have to help me cope with the inevitable withdrawal symptoms, as a sort of televisual methadone, tennis helping to wean me off an addiction to at least one live international football fixture a day.

The BBC helped to fill the short football-free void – and add to the hype – with a full-length rerun of the classic Guadalajara encounter from 1970, when England were still a genuine football superpower (and defending world champions of course). In heat and humidity which put Shizuoka in the sea-level shade, Sir Alf Ramsey's wingless wonders defended brilliantly against the likes of Pelé, Jairzinho, Rivelino, Tostao and Gerson, with Bobby Moore dominating the game like the Duke of Wellington, Winston Churchill and James Bond combined in one perfect personality. In the light of subsequent events, the miraculous one-handed save by Gordon Banks from Pelé's powerful downward header became a poignant and painful example of bulldog-spirit goalkeeping excellence. Despite losing 1–0 England still qualified for the quarter-finals, where stand-in keeper Peter

Bonetti managed to throw away a 2–0 lead for his country against the Germans – and if not for the fact that he is still alive, unlike Moore and Banks, one would have wondered if he had been reincarnated in the form of a 38-year-old with a ponytail.

The transmission of this old match on BBC Scotland caused some complaints to be registered by chippy Caledonian viewers. Vox-pop radio interviews in Scottish streets resulted in disingenuous claims by various Scots that they would have been supporting England if not for the over-the-top nationalistic coverage emanating from the London-based media. This was patent nonsense, and if you think that the English press and television were guilty of overkill coverage in their pre-showdown countdown to Shizuoka, just imagine how the Scottish media would have hyped the game if Scotland had been Brazil's opponents. A more honest position for greenly envious Scots to adopt, given that this was the first tournament for 32 years for which England had qualified and Scotland hadn't, would have been to admit that, despite having no problem with England or the English in day-to-day life or politics, most Scots just hate the living guts out of the English national football team (similar to the situation of Old Firm football fans who can work alongside and socialise with their arch-rivals personally, but who invariably succumb to feelings of loathing when watching their rivals in football action).

With the BBC and ITV sharing the broadcasting rights I once again decided on Gary Lineker & Co., since they were broadcasting *in situ* from Shizuoka Stadium. Hansen was in the expected line-up of panellists but my heart sank when I saw he was sharing what looked like a coffee table with Peter Reid and Ian Wright (who were about as capable of providing pithy analysis as Carol Smillie and Vanessa Feltz invited into a studio to comment on the results of a general election). My England shirt had been washed and ironed and I tried to wear it with 'pride'. My best friend in the whole wide world, Harvey McWilson, joined me in front of the TV to watch the game, buck bloody naked.

When the teams came out of the tunnel I was disappointed to see that Brazil were kitted out in *blue* shirts. What was the point in having the best, most attractive, most recognisable strip in the world and not wearing it in 'the unofficial World Cup final'? Could it be some stipulation in their Nike contract to wear the blue 'away' tops at least once? The bizarre white shorts worn against Costa Rica were necessary to avoid a colour clash with the opposition and if the same was true for this encounter then surely England could have reverted to all white (as in Mexico) or switched to their alternative red shirts.

Not only did Brazil not look like Brazil, they didn't play like Brazil. After a few early scares, England seemed to realise they were playing fallible human beings rather than godlike icons. In the 23rd minute a long hopeful ball fell to Lucio (who couldn't have impersonated Sol Campbell more realistically if he'd tried). Instead of whacking the ball away from danger or allowing it to run harmlessly on he attempted to control it, knocking it into the path of a grateful Owen. Marcos left his line smartly enough but made Owen's task an easy formality by going to ground before Owen had made up his mind which way to shoot. He then simply had to clip the ball over the prostrate Marcos and accept the accolades of his colleagues. England were 1–0 up and I was on my feet hopping and hollering (while McWilson looked at me stony faced).

'Thirty quid, mate. At nine-to-one.'

McWilson continued to look at me as if I was some kind of mercenary traitor.

The 20–20 hindsight critics had a field day at England's failure to launch seek-and-destroy missions for a killer second, but Plan A was working to perfection. As the Brazilian equivalent of Mexican Mariachi players were drowned out by English colliery bands playing the theme tunes from *The Great Escape* and *The Italian Job*, England just had to hang on to half time. 'Bring on Scotland', shouted some wag in the crowd (not a Brazilian, I'm sure). Flags draped around the stadium – mostly St George's but some Union Jacks – had been personalised, indicating supporters from as far afield as Carlisle and Brighton. To the strains of 'Football's Coming Home' the camera cut to conga-ing lines of English fans in the stands. It was eerily reminiscent of how Scotland fans had reacted to David Narey's 'toepoke' opener against Brazil in Spain '82. Except this Brazilian team looked like one that had struggled to qualify from their South American group.

David Seaman came for a cross, bravely out-jumping Ronaldo and doing well to hold onto the ball as he came down head first. I almost felt the judder in my own spine as he hit the ground. Some massaging with the trainer's magic sponge had him on his size-12 feet and it was almost half time.

Beckham had been rehabilitated to the point where he was now uncriticisable, which was just as well because his kangaroo jump to avoid a crunching midfield tackle from Roque Junior was less forgivable than his flick against Simeone. Petulance is one thing, physical cowardice quite another. Scholes failed to get his captain off the hook and Ronaldhino was off like the Hunchback of Notre Dame on a sexual promise from Esmeralda. A snazzy stepover and Ashley Cole was left floundering in his wake (when Cole should have been hitching a piggy-back ride if necessary to slow the Brazilian's dangerous progress). Ferdinand and Campbell both converged to block his path to goal, whereupon a flick with the outside of his boot set up the unmarked Rivaldo. The striker passed the ball into the net in *injury time* and the self-belief drained out of the English players like blood out of vampire victims. The frustration was enough to blow a cerebral gasket. The Dracula of Brazil had been there for the *staking*, but the sun set just as Sven's Van Helsings were raising their arms for the decisive blow. And then bolting upright with a horrible grin on his death-mask face had been R-R-R-Rivaldo . . .

I spent most of half-time muttering about 'bastards' (and to be honest I wasn't quite sure who were the objects of my disaffection). McWilson was pissing me off, too, just sitting there smirking.

If the ending to the first half had been like a bad dream, the start to the second was an absolute waking nightmare. Scholes gave away an unnecessary free-kick 35 yards out and Ronaldhino prepared to take it (with the Planet of the Apes mask he had insisted on wearing all through the tournament). Cafu had apparently advised him of Seaman's tendency to be caught off his line – just ask Zaragoza's Nayim, who lobbed Seaman from 50 yards in 1995 – and the Portugeuse-speaking Phantom of the Opera had spotted Seaman four yards out anticipating a cross from the right. Ronaldhino then made the decision to go for it, in the far corner, and released the Fevernova on its fateful parabola. Infringing pointlessly within ten yards of the kick, Scholes left Seaman unsighted. The goalkeeper nevertheless took another step forward when the ball was high in the air – and then stopped when he realised it was not a cross but a shot. He wasted vital nano-seconds trying to get his legs into reverse gear, but when he did his raised left arm was clutching at air. The ball dipped into the far corner and Brazil were 2–1 up, even as Seaman looked despairingly over his left shoulder before ending up in the back of the net himself.

'Gooooaaaal!' I screamed, jumping up and down and hugging McWilson. Then I stopped in mid-action, like Seaman, when I realised what I'd done (and I don't mean hugging a naked McWilson).

'Shit. I forgot. I'm supporting England . . . But what a great goal, eh?'

The Banks save against Pelé was the result of a razor-sharp mind being in perfect harmony with an athletically attuned body and he acknowledged the coaching help given by Ramsey who 'convinced me that my mind's not got to wander'. Seaman is a very good goalkeeper who suffers from occasional but disastrous lapses in concentration. At least this *faux pas* shut up the ITV panel, who had been touting Seaman for the Lev Yashin Award for goalkeeper of the tournament. The Russian was famous for his black jersey, and Seaman played this game in a black ensemble, but good old Lev was also worshipped for his phenomenal *reach*. Both commentators and most of the panellists on both channels dismissed the strike as a 'fluke' except, would you believe, Wrighty and Gazza, who correctly identified it as a genuine attempt on goal. My Scottish hackles were beginning to rise at the dissing of Ronaldhino and the stonewalling refusal to acknowledge Seaman's schoolboy culpability. If Beckham had pulled off a similar stunt, there would have been no question of it being dismissed as a flukey mis-hit cross. And if a Scottish goalkeeper had let it in, the sniggering chain reaction would have reached all the way to presenters Lineker and Lynam. Of course Ronaldhino was trying for a spectacular, if speculative, goal – like pro golfers who are always trying to hole out at par threes for holes in one. 'Nuff said, I think, although Seaman will eventually dine out on the story of this goal, after appearing in pizza commercials, for the rest of his retired life.

Eight minutes after scoring, Ronaldhino became the first scorer to be sent off in the history of the World Cup. His tackle on Mills was bright yellow but only borderline red. Mexican referee Felipe Ramos Rizo had no doubts and gave England renewed hope, although John

Motson showed some commendable objectivity when he described it as a really harsh decision (while over on ITV Clive and Big Ron were no doubt demanding the death penalty).

Merited or not, Ronaldhino's dismissal was the lucky break that should have got England back in the game. I may have cheered his 'fluke' goal but I was also cheering Ronaldhino's red card. But then a funny thing happened on the way to the final whistle: England continued to defend a 2–1 deficit against ten men! For over half-an-hour Sven-Göran Eriksson sat forlornly, wallowing in Bonapartistic defeatism, rather than exhibiting any Alexander the Greatism in his character. His team were sluggishly going through the motions, like condemned men walking to the electric chair. Thump and hope, thump and hope, thump and hope . . . Keeping possession and getting down the flanks was the obvious strategy, but captain Beckham kept dropping deeper and setting an amateurish example by hitting long balls at Brazil's three strapping central defenders, who kept looking at each other and smiling like death-row inmates who had been given full pardons by a state governor. Not one shot on target or incident of note followed the sending off. When *Owen* was withdrawn ten minutes from the end – for Darius Vassell, with Heskey left on! it was Bonapartism gone bonkers. Did Eriksson expect Prussian reinforcements for the Brazilians at any minute? Alexanderian tactics would have involved Sven getting up off his skinny arse and redirecting his troops, with Heskey, Scholes and Campbell being replaced by Fowler, Joe Cole and Martin Keown as an auxiliary-type Niall Quinn irritant up front.

Even the final whistle was a depressing anti-climax. Glorious failure is hard to take, but at least your team has made you feel tinglingly alive. Capitulating defeat just left a sense of: 'Oh, we're out . . . what a shame . . . Still, it was against mighty Brazil . . .'

I don't know what Seaman was blubbering about at the end – he hadn't just seen £300 disappearing in front of his eyes. But strangely, I was more angry at England blowing *their* best chance of ever winning the World Cup again in a foreign land. Thirty minutes of lung-bursting effort, combined with patient passing and aggressive tactics, and they could have at least taken this Brazil side into extra-time. If great saves from Marcos, goal-line clearances from Cafu and

Lucio and glaring misses from Owen and Beckham had saved Brazil, well good luck to them, but to bow out like schoolboy pupils suddenly overawed and afraid of adult masters who were mixing it up good and hard. Aach, it was a pathetic end.

Oh well, at least I wouldn't have to support England any more. Or ever again. I could switch allegiance to Brazil, the USA, Spain and *Turkey* (and please God, let them put Senegal *out* – losing £1,250 by a last-minute failure of betting nerve to punt a mere fiver on them would just be too cruel a blow to bear; honest, God, I'll do something stupid like committing a mortal sin).

I hit McWilson on the jaw – I really did, a genuine uppercut – for some out-of-order backchat after the final whistle. But since he's a blue inflatable full-size alien it didn't do him any lasting harm. Although, as I write he still isn't talking to me. As if I care. I may have my own psychological and physiological flaws, but what McWilson and a Fevernova match ball have in common is a *valve* . . .

The BBC wrapped up their coverage with a montage of pivotal moments from the game, with Oasis providing the soundtrack with 'Stop Crying Your Heart Out'.

58. Torsten Frings: the Six Million Deutschmark Man

Germany 1 USA 0
Ulsan: Friday, 21 June, 12.30 p.m., ITV

Match B: Having just lost £300 on enervated England's egress (oh, alright £30 and a *potential* jackpot of £300), I was pleased to read that the tournament's corporate advertisers were having to write off significant losses as well. According to marketing analysts Datamonitor, the shock results and premature departures of France, Argentina, Portugal and Italy had neutered the impact of advertising campaigns based around superstars like Thierry Henry, Zinedine Zidane and Luis Figo. 7Up in particular were backing a loser, after having signed up Roy Keane for £500,000 and slapped his scowling face on millions of cans of the fizzy drink (with the result that sales of 7Up in Eire plummeted to the level of Duchy of Cornwall organic wines in working-class bars by the Liffey). Fiat had devised a multi-million-lira marketing strategy featuring Francesco Totti (which might as well have been shot with Totti and Alessandro del Piero recreating the unhappy ending of *Thelma and Louise* or starring Totti as a crash-test dummy driving full-speed into a brick wall in downtown Seoul). Nike and Adidas weren't celebrating either, after recruiting 49 star strikers between them to represent their state-of-the-art surplus-value sportswear – with only seven of the signed-up sons-of-bitches managing to score a goal. Adidas's 'Footballitis' commercials concentrated on Zidane, whose thigh tendonitis had restricted him to a single ineffectual appearance. Nike's 'Uncaged' mini-movies, with 24 superstars of the pitch appearing on a derelict cargo ship, actually culminated in a hull breach which saw Figo being swept away to his doom. The accompanying Elvis Presley dirge of a theme tune, 'A Little Less Conversation', may have gone to Number One in the UK singles charts, but advertising insiders were writing the campaign off as a disaster of Titanic-esque proportions, sinking as fast as the ship shown in the commercial.

In America, the Enron shares scandal was still in full fall-out spate, but more examples of accounting malpractice would be revealed after the Germany–USA game, including blue-chip sporting sponsor Xerox overestimating profits by *billions* of dollars. But the US media were belatedly beginning to take some notice of Bruce Arena and his college boys, even if the network news shows were relegating the squad to facetious 'And finally . . .' segments. In Germany, the Teutonic Army were willing their worst football team in living memory to 'keep winning ugly'.

I was fully behind the Yanks but full of trepidation at what the Germans might inflict on them – like a robot war contested between Humvees and Panzers. It was a soccer *blitzkrieg* all right but with the Americans divebombing the German penalty area. The US bombing patterns were tight and symmetrical – and on target. Imagine Max Schelling stepping into a ring with Sugar Ray Leonard and getting a right good hiding from the smaller man. Bayer Leverkusen 'reject' Donovan was only denied a certain goal by the Hero of Ulsan Oliver Kahn, who made a phenomenal one-handed diving save. Kahn looks like something out of Wagnerian legend, a strapping blond Aryan Lohengrin (and in this match his team-mates played like swans who were trying to drown him rather than bear him away to eternal glory).

Germany managed to apply about five minutes of sustained pressure, during which US news anchors or sportscasters no doubt described Michael Ballack's goal as a 'head in'. Klose also headed against the post during this period, but 2–0 at half-time would have been a ridiculous travesty of a score-line.

In the second half, America came out fighting harder than ever. Real men may not eat pasta or drink mineral water, but along with South Korea the USA had the fittest athletes in the World Cup. They also played like soccer brain surgeons (against football hospital porters). Hippopotami are supposed to sweat blood when under extreme stress and the Germans, from first-half swan-divers, were now blundering around red-faced and puffing like hippopotami out of water and with Ernest Hemingway taking pot-shots at them with a blunderbuss.

Four minutes after the restart Gregg Berhalter finally beat Kahn with a powerful, short-range shot. The ball spun up off Kahn and was stopped from crossing the line in the Fevernova's entirety by a defender positioned at the far post. It was stopped by Torsten Frings! Using his outstretched fist. As stonewall penalties go, it was a rock-solid claim. But when the Americans implored him to point to the spot, Scottish referee Hugh Dallas was as impassive as J.R. Ewing ignoring a tearful Sue Ellen. Dallas had actually seen the handball but had decided to give Torsten Frings the benefit of the doubt with regard to his intentions! And this despite Torsten Frings having an arm suddenly shooting up at a 45-degree angle from his body! Match-summariser David Pleat commented: 'Germany benefited from a last-gasp hand-job on the line.' Steady on, David, you'll be making cracks about kerb-crawling next. Torsten Frings had just completed a six-million-pound move from Werder Bremen to Bayern Munich, but he *must* have expected a penalty award and a red card for his self-sacrificing contribution to the German cause. The US admittedly escaped punishment for a similar incident against Mexico, but the referee concerned hadn't *seen* the infringement. As an apoplectic Arena was to comment after the game: 'The big countries still get a lot more respect on calls than the smaller footballing nations.' Or as Napoleon put it: 'God is always on the side of the big battalions.' This goal-line clearance was worth the weight of Torsten Frings in gold to Germany, and then some, but if he ever gets presented with an award for it back in the Fatherland, I hope it's made of 'German silver' (a mixture of zinc and copper with no silver in it whatsoever).

Still, the US pushed for an equaliser and when Kahn came out of his penalty area to head clear, the Fevernova flew all the way to the half-way line like a V-2 rocket. US captain and Man of the Match, Reyna volleyed it straight back in an attempt at scoring with the opposing keeper off his line which made Ronaldhino's effort against England look effeminately unambitious. It missed the target by two tantalising inches.

And still the US piled forward. In the dying seconds, centre-back Tony Sanneh found himself unmarked with a glorious opportunity for a 'head in'. I reckon cramp – in his neck muscles! – prevented him from scoring, as he awkwardly headed into the side-netting.

America had not only been unlucky, they had been robbed by a refereeing blunder (although to be fair to the normally competent Dallas he was backed up by FIFA's technical committee – aka 'The Lone Gunmen' – and was awarded the fourth official honour for the final itself).

German legend Franz Beckenbauer said after watching his team reaching their *tenth* World Cup semi-final: 'If you put all our outfield players in a sack and punched it, whichever player you hit would deserve it.' He didn't single out Torsten Frings for a special punishment beating, but if I was an American I'd have loved to kick his ass from Ulsan to Seoul. Torsten Frings had denied the USA their *second*-ever semi-final place in a World Cup (after getting there in 1930 in Uruguay, where they lost 6–1 to Argentina).

What can you say about the Germans? Anything you bloody well like. They don't care and it won't stop them winning *häblich*.

59. 'Hiddinkism' Declared State Religion

Spain 0 South Korea 0
Gwangju: Saturday, 22 June, 7.30 a.m., BBC

Match C: As the luxury air-conditioned coach carrying the Spanish squad towards Gwangju Stadium, 200 miles south of Seoul, hit the outskirts of the city, every street along the route was lined by screaming South Koreans. Almost every single one sported a red T-shirt emblazoned with the slogan 'Be the Reds'. President Kim Dae-Jung, who attended the game for the political photo-opportunities it offered, had ordered a sweep of the streets to remove any undesirable elements from public view (such as beggars, prostitutes and fast-food sellers specialising in canine catering). The Spaniards must have felt like modern conquistadors, massively outnumbered but politely welcomed by the trusting natives. But unlike Cortes and Pizarro, who were accepted as all powerful (if murdering) gods, Morientes and Hierro knew that when footballing battle commenced they were going to have to fight tooth and nail for a positive result (and without the injured Raúl¹ to help get the goals required for progression to the semi-final).

The stamina and speed of the South Koreans had prompted allegations of drug abuse, but Hiddink had spent months honing his charges to physical perfection in a specially constructed boot camp near the DMZ (and although the players were rewarded for reaching the second round with exemptions from military service, it could be argued that they had already gone through a fitness regime that would have qualified them for the South Korean SAS). It was Formula One football once again, cheered on by 43,000 supporters who sounded as if they were on Class A stimulants. Spain soaked up the early pressure and even reached half-time disappointed not to be ahead.

Early in the second half, Ivan Helguerra rose with Kim Tae-Yong for a dangerous cross and the South Korean stopper deflected the ball into his own net. It looked a perfectly legitimate goal, from every replayed angle, but Egyptian referee Gamal Ghandour blew for a mysterious infringement. The look he got from Helguerra could have felled a Pamplona charging bull from 20 yards away. Morientes hit the post and squandered chances before red-haired substitute Lee Chun-Soo came on to torment the Spanish defence. The 0–0 scoreline at full-time flattered the home side, but they hadn't stopped running and shooting on sight of goal for the full 90 minutes.

In extra-time, Raúl's replacement, Joaquin, got to the by-line and flighted over a perfect cross for Morientes to head home an easy Golden Goal. Except it was chalked off by the referee, after he spotted Trinidadian linesman Michael Ragoonath with his flag raised. For what, offside? No way, José. In fact, he'd signalled for a goal-kick, believing that the ball had gone out of play before Joaquin had been able to cross. Replays showed conclusively that the Fevernova had barely touched the white line, never mind crossed it in its entirety. Not surprisingly, Spain began to play like paranoid schizophrenics convinced that the world and his South Korean brother were all against them. South Korea sighed in relief, shrugged their shoulders and got on with the job of running Spain ragged.

Facing a penalty shoot-out, the Spaniards lined up as if facing a firing squad. The South Koreans prepared like a firing squad, one so sadistically relishing the prospect that they collectively declined the traditional one blank cartridge for one of their unknowing number.

It's not a myth that Orientals tend to be more short-sighted than Occidentals, and hence more likely to need spectacles, but it is a myth that the South Koreans are more 'slanty eyed' than their Spanish opponents. They aren't – they simply have nose bridges which are lower, combined with Mongolian folds of the upper eyelids. This genetic combination gives the appearance of 'slanted eyes' (and sadly some young Oriental women actually pay for plastic surgery to make them look more 'Western'[1]).

All the penalties were converted until at 4–3 Joaquin limped upfield to take his. The 20-year-old not only appeared injured, he looked extremely nervous. Lee Woon-Jae dived the right way – left – and parried the shot away two-handedly, but the South Korean goalkeeper was at least a yard off his line when the kick was struck. It was so blatant an infringement that even I spotted it in real-time viewing. But no retake was ordered and home captain Hong Myung-Bo stepped up to blast the ball past Casillas.

South Korea won 5–3 on penalties and secured a place in the *semi-finals*.

Spain took defeat even worse than the Italians had, with some players having to be restrained from physically remonstrating with the match officials.

Judging by some of the post-match quotes, the Spanish seriously seemed to believe that referees selected for matches involving South Korea had been bribed or blackmailed – combined with home players being intravenously fed with liquid steroids during half-time breaks. Hiddink advised the Spanish to go look in a mirror, suggesting that they had no one to blame but themselves. The thought of Masonic conspiracy did cross my mind, since Spain had joined Poland, Portugal and Italy as high-class Catholic scalps.

South Korea had benefited from some highly dubious decisions, yes; that was undeniable, but what were they supposed to do in such circumstances? They may have been riding their outrageous luck, but how could you hold it against them if fortune, for once, really was favouring the brave?

After the game one Scottish sports commentator on a local radio station suggested that South Korea versus Brazil in the Big Yo would be a dream final, forecasting that the passionate support for the 'home team' might even be enough to unsettle the South Americans. Yes, well, I was almost tempted to phone in. The Japanese were highly unlikely to switch support from their favourite second team to their overachieving arch-rival neighbours (and looking at a map I was surprised to see that almost a quarter of Japan lies further south in latitude than the South Korean equivalent of Land's End).

Production of Guus Hiddink dolls must have gone into industrial overdrive to satisfy demand. If South Korea were fated to win this World Cup, Hiddinkism would have to be added to the main religions of Animism, Buddhism and Confucianism. If he didn't watch his step, he could have found himself being declared 'divine' and refused permission to leave the country until he had succeeded in reuniting the North and South. And to think if Leicester City's Martin O'Neill had said no to managing Glasgow Celtic, Hiddink could have been overseeing pre-season training in Largs instead of coaching his World Cup minnows to further glory.

NOTES

[1] Why any woman, or man, would want to look more 'Western' is beyond me. Northern European Caucasian has to be the least aesthetically attractive racial configuration of facial features, physique and skin on the planet. Especially in the form of overweight carrot-tops from the central belt of Scotland.

60. The Young Turk and the Bosphorus Bull

Senegal 0 Turkey 1
Osaka: Saturday, 22 June, 12.30 p.m., ITV

Match D: As soon as the Spain–South Korea quarter-final finished, I began to worry obsessively about the outcome of Senegal–Turkey. I squirmed at the prospect of 'losing' over a thousand pounds if the Senegalese succeeded in stringing together three more wins. That unpunted fiver was playing havoc with my psychological peace of mind. If they actually reached the final, it would be National Lottery non-purchase regret syndrome all over again (when I *once* failed to play my regular six numbers and watched the televised draw in genuine and growing horror as the first three balls drawn by Lancelot or Guinevere matched half of my regular numbers, which thankfully only cost me a tenner but if the sequence had continued it could have resulted in full-on, on-the-spot suicide). I needed whisky to get through the last quarter-final, but not the ulcerous explosions of red-hot poker pain if I knocked back a bottle of cheap supermarket grain whisky without something to protect my stomach-lining. Since I didn't have any Pepto-Bismal left, I decided to outfox my digestive system with Warnink's Advocaat as a mixer. It worked like a dream, with no doubling over in agony, not to mention the silver lining of the additional alcoholic buzz.

At kick-off John Champion commented on the powerful physique of the Africans – and the six foot plus super-athletes of Senegal did resemble a Nubian Honour Guard in the court of Cleopatra (and a Taiwanese hotel proprietor had complained publicly about their allegedly hiring 37 prostitutes during a pre-tournament stopover on the island). By comparison the Turkish midfield quartet of Sas, Emre, Basturk and Tuguay were pygmie-esque in height and build. I took some hope from the fact that while the whole Senegalese team played for provincial French clubs like Souchaux, Rennes, Montpellier, Lens, Monaco, Lorrient and Auxerre, Turkey had key players plying their club trade with the likes of AC Milan (Davala), Parma (Sukur), Bayer Leverkusen (Basturk), Inter Milan (Emre!), Blackburn Rovers (Tugay) and Aston Villa (Alpay). In keeper Rustu they had the only genuine challenger to Oliver Kahn for the Lev Yashin Award.

As the tight game progressed, it was obvious that Senegal had shot their bolt as an attacking force. Conversely, they were defending with such brute force and passionate commitment that Turkey must have felt they were knocking their heads against a big black brick wall. Athletic interceptions, and one goal-line clearance from Daf, were frustrating Turkey – to say nothing of the form of non-scoring centre-forward Hakan Sukur. The Bull of the Bosphorus was in a state of psychological castration, a lumbering liability up front whose inept performance was in danger of demoralising his team-mates. Sas set him up for a tap-in sitter, but Sukur couldn't even make contact with his studs as the ball squirmed under his foot and away. His ego may have been as inflated as normal, but his confidence was visibly draining away, to the point where the chances that were being created for him by hard-working colleagues sweating blood were causing him to break out in cold sweats of anxiety. Sukur was also the leader of the Muslim faction in the squad, his insistence on praying with an Iman irritating the more secular players.

Coach Senol Gunes was on the horns of a dilemma, having to calculate the amount of rope he could play out to his star striker before tieing a knot for a noose and hauling him off. Sukur is a national hero in Turkey; his wedding was televised live to a grateful nation (and to be fair, his goals had helped Turkey to qualify for the tournament). If Gunes withdrew him for the highly-rated Ihan Mansiz of Besikatas, Turkey were a lot more likely to snatch a winner; however, replacing him and going on to lose the match would have seen Gunes being crucified in the Turkish media, not to mention being spat at on the streets of Istanbul. Turkish football fans are almost psychotically passionate about their clubs and country, whether it be the Old Firm intensity of hatred between Galatasary and Fenerbahce or the 'Welcome to Hell' banners which greet teams arriving for away fixtures in the Champions League or UEFA Cup. Indeed, when Rustu had kept goal for Fenerbahce in a Turkish Cup final and they had lost to an *amateur* team, the goalkeeper had been dragged from his Mercedes and beaten up by furious Fenerbahce fans.

Gunes waited until the 67th minute before bowing to the tactically inevitable substitution. Sukur stomped off and Mansiz bounded on with all the self-belief and enthusiasm of a 25-year-old who had finished as the highest scorer in the Turkish league. Within minutes, his audacious lob almost beat Tony Sylva with the ball landing on the roof of the net.

Senegal dug in to earn the reprieve of Golden Goal extra time, by which time I was happily drunk. The thought of an arbitrary, stop-dead Golden Goal for Senegal sobered me up, though, and they had already succeeded in scoring one against Sweden, of course . . .

I needn't have hit the sweet sherry stored under the sink, because within three minutes Davala's distinctive Mohican was bombing down the right wing. His cross was met on the half-volley by Mandiz, sweeping the ball into the far corner with all the *sang froid* of a striker showing off in a bounce game . . .

A Golden Goal 1–0 win for Turkey, then, sending Senegal back home at the same stage of the tournament as Cameroon reached in Italia '90. I was celebrating like a citizen of Constantinople, where the mobile-phone system crashed as Turks communicated with each other over the airwaves to belt out spontaneous renditions of 'May Our Hearts Rejoice'.

I passed out as Gunes ran out onto the pitch, thinking that the smartly-suited coach was the most sartorially elegant manager in the competition, along with Rudi Völler in his light grey two-piece.[1]

NOTES

[1] 'Hello, Mum, it's me . . . Yeah, I'm phoning on my new *mobile*. I'm in Marks and Sparks in Princes Street, buying my second-ever brand new suit . . . It's a smart grey two-piece for the Booker ceremony . . . No, not high fashion with a high V at the front. More traditional, but still cool – think Graham Greene hero in light cotton for summer in the tropics . . . Blue shirt, brushed cotton . . . sort of Brooks Brothers with button-down collar . . . Tie? Dunno – like Gunes? Or just open-necked casual like Völler? Gotta go, incoming

call . . . Hello . . . Well hi, Ms Paltrow . . . Okay, Gwyneth . . . Thanks, I thought *Last Train to Timbuctoo* was a good title too . . . well, actually nothing's signed as such but I did promise the female lead to Kylie. It was written with her in mind . . . A shoo-in for an Oscar . . . Yeah, I'm sure it will be if I don't fuck up the direction . . . Yes I am . . . The English schoolteacher who goes mad in the desert . . . yeah, I'm sure you could do the accent and if you want that supporting role, you've got it . . . Married? Me? No . . . Gay? Certainly not . . . No, not at all . . . Well obviously I'd not be too happy if one married my sister . . . Funny guy, for sure . . . Creative genius – dunno about that . . . Okay, get your people to talk to my probation officer . . . She handles all that shit . . . See ya soon, baby . . . Mum, ya ain't gonna believe who I was just fielding a phone call from . . . talking like goddam what? Schmuck, yourself, Ma . . . I'm on top of the world, Ma, on top of the goddam world . . .'

Ring-trill. Ring-trill. Ring-trill . . .

'Hello, Mum . . . Oh, not so great. I've got a really bad hangover . . . Love you, too but I've got to go . . . Appointment with Mr Armitage Shanks . . . Bye.'

BAAAAARRRRRFFFFFF.

'Okay, Mr Spielberg, this is the pitch . . . You're in a fatal car crash. Or whatever . . . A light appears and you're floating towards it . . . Then you wake up in this big arena, filled with thousands of seats . . . Like the spectators assembled to watch the trial for David Niven's soul in Powell and Pressburger's *A Matter of Life and Death* . . . you take a Pullman seat in the middle, then loved ones and friends sit beside and around you . . . Then everyone you've *ever* met fills all the rest of the seats . . . The lights dim and a giant screen flickers into life . . . it shows your whole life in real time, from the moment of your birth until your death . . . Everything you've ever done, even behind closed doors, and everything you've ever said . . . Plus every thought you've ever had is up there on subtitles . . . Split-screen zooms in on audience members for reaction shots whenever they are involved, like when slagging people off behind their backs. Well, it ends with your death up on the screen and then continual re-runs of your fucked-up life for eternity . . . It's my idea of hell too, Mr Spielberg . . . Just get your people to call my probation officer . . .'

61. The Good German Ballack

Germany 1 South Korea 0
Seoul: Tuesday, 25 June, 12.30 p.m., ITV

The first semi-final was relying on the Germans to restore some order to a tournament that was in danger of descending into form-book anarchy. Quickly reminding myself of the German record so far (8–0, 1–1, 2–0, 1–0 and 1–0), I remembered to give them some extra credit for the thrashing of Saudi Arabia (since this dictatorial monarchy still harboured that cuddliest of characters Idi Amin and had refused to alter its constitution, even after the Gulf War, to permit women to drive in public). Trying to think of an example of modern cultural production from a unified Germany that I had enjoyed, I suddenly remembered the TV series *Heimat* from the early '90s, a sort of democratic socialist soap-opera, *Peyton Place* with scowling squareheads in the fictional town of Sabbach. The sequel *The New Generation* was even better, combining the production values of *Brideshead Revisited* with a Teutonic *Twin Peaks* sensibility. And *Magic Hoffman* was a good literary novel with some genuine laughs, whose author would deserve a namecheck if my mental retrieval system weren't in dire need of re-booting. In the sporting arena, the imperial Michael Schumacher was still getting heavy flak for following team orders and overtaking Ferrari team-mate Rubens Barricello (who had been ordered to move over and slow down), for an undeserved Formula One victory in Austria. The only reason I could think of for visiting Germany as a tourist was the opportunity to drive round the Nuremburg Ring racing circuit in your own car, for a fee of £7 and after signing an insurance disclaimer. In contemporary politics, head of state Herr Schröder was still threatening to sue if the German media continued to 'libel' him with damaging allegations about using hair dye to maintain his youthful image . . .

Even taking all the above into account, I couldn't help but hope that the South Korean fairytale would continue.

The Germans came out and entertained the red sea of semi-hysterical South Korean supporters with group callisthenics, before forming a human pyramid for their national anthem. As 'Deutschland Über Alles' belted out of the P.A. system, they looked into the hand-held camera with square-jawed determination and wet-eyed sentimentality. The South Koreans looked like adrenaline junkies blissing out on another hit.

Lee Chun-Soo should have scored early on, but Kahn dived like a nuclear-powered U-boat and palmed the powerful shot clear with a strong wrist. The Germans then began to run the game like middle managers in charge of a ball-bearing factory in Stuttgart. Timetable tactics and scientific management soccer skills completely neutralised the South Korean threat and for the first time in the competition that hoary old myth about Asians not being able to play professional football looked to have an element of truth to it. They may have been struggling to get their zoom football out of neutral but it wasn't due to lack of effort. Hundreds of Red Devils in the two-tier stands were wearing Guus Hiddink masks, and although the Germans hadn't silenced the 64,000 home support a German oompah-oompah band could occasionally be heard through the background static chanting of 'Dae Ha Min Guk' ('Come on Korea'?).

Clive Tyldsley got in the first gratuitous reference to Eng-ur-lund when he reminded ITV viewers that 'this German team is just a few hundred days away from their mauling by Michael [Owen] and Company'. Two hundred and ninety-eight days, to be precise, from the fateful 5–1 victory in Munich, after which Sven-Göran Eriksson descended the airplane steps at Luton Airport flapping the piece of paper which promised 'World Cup victory in our time'.

In the 70th minute, Torsten Frings totally fucked up in midfield and as Lee Chun-Soo zeroed in on the penalty box Michael Ballack tripped him up. The booking prevented Ballack from appearing in the final, if Germany got there, but no Gazzaesque tears flowed. Ballack insisted later that he had 'no bad feelings' towards Torsten Frings and his coach Völler complimented the midfielder on his 'absolutely necessary tactical foul'. Like Seven-of-One in *Star Trek: Voyager*, who had once been assimilated by the Borg Collective, Ballack got on with the game for the good of team-mates and country. Bearing a remarkable resemblance to First Officer Chakotay, he started a lung-bursting run from deep four minutes after being booked. Neuville, a Neelix look-a-like, dribbled down the right wing like an Alsatian whippet. His cross found Ballack, whose right foot shot was blocked by Communications Officer Harry Kim. Switching feet for the rebound, Ballack slotted home the opener and winner.

'A deafening silence,' mourned Clive. The South Koreans got their vocal chords working again and settled back to enjoy yet another last-gasp equaliser, Golden Goal extra time and penalty shoot-out success. But this was Germany they were playing, whose footballers are almost genetically programmed to sit on 1–0 leads. The majority of their home internationals are played at Hamburg's Volksparkstadion, which instead of an athletics or greyhound track is surrounded by a particle accelerator. Whether this affects the players when switched on during games is a moot point, but I'm sure they have researched the possibility.

Tears flowed at the final whistle, as the Red Devils faced up to the reality of football supporting: eventual failure and crushing disappointment. But unlike the Japanese, they soon bounced back, cheering and clapping as their team took their honourable leave.

As the Germans congratulated themselves (which, let's face it, no one else was going to do) and packed up their kit for the flight to Japan, the South Koreans stayed behind in the stadium clearing up their own rubbish and depositing it in big bin bags. The main party may have been over, gatecrashed by the squareheads, but they had a third-place play-off to look forward to. The rest of us had the Germans in yet another final to look forward to. '*Gawdelpus,*' as Goethe once remarked.

Maybe I'd watch *Heimat* on video instead. Karl-Heinz Rummenigge really was excellent in it. Or swallow half a dozen German marching pills in the form of amphetamine methedrine.

62. Samba Boys Go Schizo in Saitama

Brazil 1 Turkey 0
Saitama: Wednesday, 26 June, 12.30 p.m., BBC

The second semi-final saw a second confrontation between Brazil and Turkey. Eh? The two qualifying teams from each group are normally split into different sides of the draw so that they cannot meet again before the final. The Sweden–England game had indeed included references to a possible semi-final re-match. What the hell was going on? I eventually figured it out – because of the co-host sharing of this World Cup such potential re-meetings became logistically inevitable. Why? Well, with Japan and South Korea pencilled in for permanent home fixtures and with no other team being required to 'move countries' more than once before the final, the draw had been 'fixed' (or massaged). Since Turkey and Brazil had both qualified from South Korea's Group C and henceforth played their knockout games in Japan, neither could be expected to switch back to South Korea for a semi-final. Turkey had surpassed all expectations, including their own, but they were up for revenge after the controversial 2–1 defeat in Ulsan three weeks earlier. Brazil certainly weren't underestimating the Turks after their first harem-scarem meeting, but they must have been fairly confident of giving them a reality check in the form of a heavy defeat.

Germany had kept the flag flying for Adidas against Nike-sponsored South Korea, and 'Team Nike' in the form of Brazil were firm favourites to dispose of Adidas-kitted Turkey.

'OK' may be the most recognisable word in the world, but the second is 'Coca-Cola'. Pepsi must languish somewhere down in the nether-regions of name recognition, despite having signed up Michael Jackson in the past and featuring David Beckham in World Cup commercials playing footie against Sumo wrestlers. Scotland is the only country in the world in which an indigenous soft drink like Irn-Bru outsells Coke. Ironically, Coca-Cola was invented by a Scottish doctor called John Pemberton, a morphine junkie whose 'nerve tonic' originally contained cocaine as part of its mythical '7X' formula (which today is nothing but a cocktail of coriander, cinnamon, nutmeg and orange extracts). Personally I just drop a couple of Dif 118s into a can of Coke to give it an old-fashioned kick. In the high-profile corporate marketing wars, Coke versus Pepsi now plays second fiddle to Adidas versus Nike. But unlike Pepsi, new boys on the block Nike managed to surpass Adidas in sales as early as 1979, thanks to a combination of big-budget marketing and 'rebel advertising'. This extraordinary phenomenon actually targets trend-setting teenagers and sells to them with the paradoxical promise that 'if you buy from us, you will be reinforcing your own uniqueness'. Nike in 1994, for example, used the rebel-without-an-accidentally-killed-wife William Burroughs to front a campaign for Air Max sneakers. The wrinkled old Beat poet, homosexual and heroin addict was not universally recognised by mall rats with their own store cards and comfortable Mid Western suburban homes, but he gave an 'underground edge' to the brand. I always knew the author of *The Naked Lunch* (which is literally unreadable) would end up selling out to corporate America, even with an enigmatic smile and ironic shoulder-shrugging, but it's fellow Beat writer Jack Kerouac I feel sorry for. Kerouac must have turned in his early grave when The Gap commandeered his photographic image for their 'Kerouac/Dean/Monroe wore khakis' campaign. Pepsi actually paid *millions* to the organisers of Woodstock '94 to ensure that theirs was the only soft-drinks logo to appear at the festival, as cynical an act as Nike buying up Brazil and rebranding them 'Team Nike'.

The problem in post-modern, morally-relative, quote-unquote contemporary society is that no famous artists – no matter how *avant garde*, experimental, offensive or outright psychotic – can stop themselves or their work being subsumed into the mainstream culture because, in part, of cynical advertisers who will hijack any outsider, no matter how extreme or radical, in order to appeal to media-savvy 'young people'. Kerouac's *On the Road* really is frenetic typing rather than inspired writing, but at least he wasn't stopping off in shopping malls en route to stock up on beige khakis, cargo pants and one-pocket T-shirts, all with designer labels. If the Marquis de Sade were alive today he would probably be signed up by Victoria's Secret or Dateline.

The 'Just Do It' exploitation of Ronaldo can be traced back to Nike's endorsement by top basketball stars in the mid-1980s, such as Michael Jordan. This commercialisation of sport and its icons, resulting in couch-potato consumers buying Nike for their 'implied performance benefits', almost bankrupted Adidas, before they started to make massive profits too in the 1990s by aping the Nike strategy of the 1980s and spinning their stuck-in-70s-groove image into retro-chic desirability. Founded by German athlete Adi Dassler in 1920, by the 1970s their triple stripes transformed ordinary T-shirts into high-value fashion items and ordinary trainers into objects of foot-fashion desire. The Nike swoosh may have slaughtered the Adidas stripes in the '80s but by 2002 both symbols have brand recognition that independent sportswear manufacturers can only dream about (or dream about ripping off in fake versions, a practice which has both Nike and Adidas self-righteously screaming in unison and hiring corporate lawyers right, left and centre to protect their products' 'purity').

Enough already, I know, but just for the record all my trainers (or sneakers) for the past 20 years have been Hi-Tech, a brand which sells for about a third of the price of better-known brands. Come to think of it, in the vomit-inducingly sentimental *The Big Chill*, Kevin Kline's character was subtextually pigeon-holed as a sell-out phoney because his baby-boomer past as a revolutionary radical had been betrayed by his transmogrification into a self-employed businessman making and selling sports shoes.

But to be completely honest, approaching my last birthday on a shopping expedition with my mum in the St Enoch shopping mall, we both spotted a pair of Adidas trainers in a shop window reduced from £69.99 to £29.99. They were a beautiful brushed cotton blue, with the three trademark stripes and I fell in love with them at first sight. But they turned out to be a size 11 and I would have fallen out of them if I'd as much as broken into a light jog. I left the discount shoe store blinking away tears of consumer frustration . . . Who needs 'Awidas' I thought later, giggling at the picture of the triangular trefoil redesigned as a pot leaf logo, but frowning at a TV commercial for Munchie Bites (some kind of snack being pushed by rebel advertisers aiming at the midnight munching market!). At least Senegal had a cool kit sponsor, Le Coq Sportif, which hopefully doesn't have sweatshop slaves running up shirts for a few francs an hour in the ex-colony (or maybe that would be a good thing, providing employment and a living wage for women who would otherwise be starving).

In a vastly superior game to Germany–South Korea, Brazil were far from brilliant but they weren't half bad by their own high standards. Turkey played well, too, going for victory but coming up against a bizarrely back-to-front Brazil, who defended terrifically, were dangerous from midfield but who lacked punch up front. The game was decided by two contrasting efforts by Ronaldo and Sukur, the former toe-poking his way to fortuitous goal-scoring glory and the latter displaying a strike of belated technical brilliance which if anything was struck too sweetly to trouble a relieved Marcos in the Brazilian goal.

By the 49th minute, Ronaldo's injury-prone body and despair-inclined mind seemed to be combining to return him to the shadow of his former, pre-tournament self. Stiff in movement and slow in mind, Big Phil must have been considering substituting the up-until-now rejuvenated wreck from France '98. He had certainly lured the Turkish defence into a false sense of security, without the suspended Ronaldhino to play the ball to his silver-booted feet, but he picked the ball up in no man's land and was suddenly striding into the Turkish penalty box. Three red-shirted defenders were about to descend on him like *Rollerball* players, and almost certainly dispossess him, when he flicked his right leg and sent the ball skimming towards the far post. The surprise element in his decision to shoot – borne from physical exhaustion and/or psychological desperation? – wrong-footed Rustu and, although he got an outstretched glove on it, the Fevernova continued its crawl-like progress towards the net. Once again a slightly mis-hit or partly sclaffed shot had proved more difficult for a good goalkeeper to deal with than a sweetly-struck but predictable effort.

In the 80th minute, Sas flighted a free-kick towards the far corner where Sukur spun his marker and allowed the ball to drop over his head. Turning into the volley, having mentally calculated where the dropping ball would be, he caught the Fevernova with full-on, fervid force and it bulleted towards the roof of the net. Marcos, however, was properly positioned – which is half the secret of being a good keeper – and palmed it to safety with relative ease. If Sukur had not connected with such admirable precision and timing he would probably have scored a, say, 75 per cent successful connection diverting the ball away from its expected course by 25 per cent – and thereby requiring a save of outstanding reflexes and agility to stop it going in. At the death, Roberto Carlos tried some fancy footwork at right-back and needlessly lost possession to terrier-like Sas. The bald little buzz-bomb hit the by-line and crossed invitingly for substitute Mansiz, who had arrived a nano-second too early and was stretching backwards for the header, which whipped over the post by a matter of inches. Big Phil on the touchline looked as if he was sending the smiling and unconcerned Carlos telepathic death threats.

The BBC coverage had once again 'benefited' from a studio located in the stadium. Ian Wright's solipsistically shambling contributions to previous debates were forgotten and forgiven when he delivered a killer comment on Sukur's overdue wait for a goal: 'They might have to induce him.' Nice one, Ian, cancel the frontal lobotomy. Lineker signed off with the following observation about the Brazil–Germany final: 'Difficult to know who to root for really . . .'

63. Four Sailors Dead Before Fastest Goal

South Korea 2 Turkey 3
Daegu: Saturday, 29 June, 12 noon, ITV

Just when you thought it was safe to go back in the water beside the Disneyfied DMZ, a naval exchange of fire between North and South Korean vessels left four sailors from the South dead. Unification will ultimately become a reality, but before then more people will almost certainly lose their lives in border skirmishes. A few hours after this firefight at sea, the third-place play-off kicked off. Normally these games are tepid anti-climaxes but 64,000 South Koreans were back on supporting duty to give their new national heroes one last blast of patriotic support.

The players on both sides must have allowed their thoughts to drift to what-might-have-been scenarios of a different dream final (or nightmare depending on your corporate or personal point of view). South Korean captain Hong Myung-Bo must have been grateful that this fixture *wasn't* an alternative reality World Cup final, because the retiring 33-year-old veteran played his disastrous part in producing the fastest ever goal in the history of the tournament. Straight from kick-off, South Korea back-passed to Myung-Bo, who was caught daydreaming in possession by the marauding and hyped-up Mansiz. His out-of-nowhere tackler squared the ball to Sukur, who side-footed professionally into the open goal. The goal came after 10.8 seconds and ITV showed numerous replays with a ticking digital clock in the corner of the screen. The previous fastest goal had been scored by Czechoslovakia's Vaclav Masek against Mexico in 1962 (although this interesting and relevant piece of information wasn't provided by ITV, needless to say).

With the pressure off, South Korea finally lived down to pre-tournament expectations. Their three-man defence played as if struck deaf, dumb and blind. Combined with Sukur and Mansiz starting a game together for the first time – a pairing that must have had the Turks wishing they'd deployed it against Brazil – South Korea appeared in danger of finishing their fairytale story with a drubbing of nightmare proportions. However, they equalised from a free-kick before Mansiz struck twice before the break. An injury-time consolation goal came too late to engender any real doubt about the outcome and the Turks tucked third-place bronze medals into their kit-bags. Before departing the field of play, Sukur initiated a hand-holding line of players from both sides and they all bowed to the wildly cheering crowd.

The besuited Hiddink was thrown high by his grateful players, punching the air in vindication as he rose and fell. South Korea were officially the fourth-best football team in the world. Bronze medallists Turkey flew home to a heroes' welcome too, F-16 fighter jets escorting them once their airliner had entered Turkish airspace. In Istanbul, massive crowds congregated to show their appreciation as the players moved round the city streets in an open-topped bus. A massive fireworks display lit up the night sky and this cityscape must have been a sight well worth seeing on such a night.

South Korea had had a glimpse of how horribly wrong this tournament could have turned out for them, but they had fought for their undoubted good fortune and thoroughly deserved fourth place (which Scotland would settle for just once, in any of the 21st century's remaining World Cups).

Honour satisfied on both sides, then, in this entertaining match, with a mouth-watering finale in the Big Yo to look forward to . . .

64. Brazil Detonate Nuclear Bomb in the Big Yo

Brazil 2 Germany 0
Yokohama: Sunday, 29 June, 12 noon, BBC and ITV

After all the shocks and surprises in this World Cup of über-underdogs, the final still resulted in a clash of titans between Planet Football's two historical superpowers. Since the Second World War only one final had been contested without the presence of Brazil or Germany – 1978's Argentina–Holland game – but amazingly Brazil and Germany had never met at any stage of the competition. Both had appeared in seven finals, with Brazil winning four and Germany three. The Brazilian team of 2002 had reached this showdown deservedly but without touching the heights of true greatness achieved by their predecessors, while Germany had ridden their luck and managed to avoid the pratfalls that had befallen pre-tournament favourites like France and Argentina (and Italy and Portugal, who had been seeded to meet Germany instead of the USA and South Korea). Oliver Kahn had already collected the Golden Gloves award for best goalkeeper even before kick-off (with 18 goal-saving stops). Miroslav Klose, Rivaldo and Ronaldo were all in contention for the Golden Shoe award for most prolific goal-scorer. This final would be remembered for the contrasting fortunes of Kahn and Ronaldo (but not in the expected way, with great saves from the former and even greater goals from the latter).

On Sunday, 12 July 1998, Brazil had had an early lunch in their Paris hotel before their players retired to their rooms to prepare mentally for that afternoon's final against hosts France. Ronaldo, who had the hopes of a football crazy and utterly expectant nation resting on his broad but young shoulders, succumbed to some kind of fit, shaking from head to toe, frothing at the mouth and lapsing into unconsciousness. One fast-thinking team-mate used a finger to make sure Ronaldo did not swallow his tongue. After the fit ran its worrying course, the 21-year-old striker promptly fell asleep.

Hurried consultations amongst squad doctors, team management and fellow players ended with a decision to wake Ronaldo and tell him what had just happened. While the rest of the squad rode on the team coach to the Stade de France, Ronaldo was rushed to a private clinic for emergency tests. With less than an hour to go before kick-off, a team-sheet was released without Ronaldo selected to play. He then arrived in the Brazilian dressing room insisting that he felt fine and that all the tests had proved negative. As Ronaldo was reinstated on the paperwork listing the Brazilian starting 11, confusion reigned amongst the world's assembled media (and I remember being hunched over in front of my black-and-white TV wondering what the hell was going on).

Brazil, of course, crashed to a 3–0 defeat, with Ronaldo putting in an understandably below-par performance. At the final whistle, French celebrations coincided with the start of conspiracy theories that began to multiply exponentially. Had Ronaldo suffered a nervous and/or physical breakdown due to the enormous pressures of expectation that he was having to deal with? Was he suffering from a secret or undiagnosed neurological condition? Or had he been nobbled like a race horse, doped by French secret servicemen dressed as chambermaids?

In retrospect, the decision to play Ronaldo was medically foolhardy and unethical, because a second fit in the heat of footballing battle could conceivably have resulted in his premature death. In any other circumstances, or with any other player, the patient would have been kept in hospital overnight for observation. Scapegoats for the decision ranged from Nike representatives determined to get their investment into action to members of the Brazilian Football Confederation desperate to get their best player on the pitch. Following a parliamentary investigation in Brazil, which Ronaldo attended in person to give evidence, the likeliest explanation of the above murky events would appear to be a team doctor who administered an anaesthetic to deaden the pain in a troublesome knee. The pharmaceutical compound then reacted badly in Ronaldo's system, his metabolism coping with the foreign bodies by inducing an epileptic fit. The team management then decided to risk playing him because he seemed to have recovered with no obvious ill effects and was indispensable to Brazil's hopes of winning.

Whatever the cause, and whoever was responsible (if anyone), Ronaldo had to endure almost four years of hurt, both physical and psychological, as he underwent extensive and repeated knee surgery, combined with other injuries which threatened to end his club career with Inter Milan. Numerous attempted comebacks ended in physical breakdowns and in season 2001–02 he only managed seven goals for the Italian giants. His selection for the Brazil squad was a calculated risk by Scolari, at the expense of Romario losing his place, but, as with Eriksson and Beckham, the Brazil coach hoped that 80 per cent fitness would improve as the tournament progressed.

Germany may have been fortunate to find themselves contesting another final, but their Bayer Leverkusen players in particular must have been hoping that Dame Fortune would continue to smile in their direction. Oliver Neuville, Carsten Ramelow and Bernd Schneider (not to mentioned the recently transferred but suspended Michael Ballack) had starred for the eternal losers and perennial bottlers of German club football in a season that started like a dream but ended like a nightmare. In quick succession they had thrown away a comfortable lead to lose the Bundesliga title on the last day of the season (to Borussia Dortmund), then lost the German Cup final 4–2 (to Schalke), before completing this miserable hat-trick by losing the European Cup final at Hampden Park 2–1 (to Real Madrid). A fourth final-fence *faux pas* in a World Cup final would be very hard to take.

Keeper Kahn had, of course, had to come to terms with picking the ball out of the net five times against England. In addition he had been between the Bayern Munich posts in 1999, when Manchester United snatched the European Cup with two cruelly late goals in injury time. In Germany, an alternative comedian had christened him 'Kahn the Gorilla' and at some away games he had to endure the indignity of opposing fans throwing bananas at him. (Football fans: don't ya just love 'em sometimes?).

All these, and other untold back-stories, came together for an exciting final chapter at 12 noon in the Yokohama International Stadium.

John Motson had beaten Barry Davies for the honour of commentating for Auntie Beeb – yawn, I know, as if anyone cared and as if either of them weren't sheepskin-coat-wearing bourgeois bores, broadcasting dinosaurs who ought to have been put out to grass years ago – along with co-commentator Trevor Brooking (who really has fallen on his retired footballing feet with this sinecure of a job, the main requirement of which seems to be getting through 90 broadcast minutes without saying anything controversial or even interesting). The thought of Clive Tyldsley and Ron Atkinson over on ITV was just too awful to even contemplate switching over, what with their 1950s-style vaudeville act.

Aaarrrgggghhh!!!! Brazil turned out in their traditional strip, except for sporting *blue* socks. Why weren't Germany forced to replace their white socks instead? During the national anthems, Ronaldo looked like Bugs Bunny mesmerised by Elmer Fudd's approaching headlights, as he rocked nervously from one foot to the other. Kahn was as impressive and impassive as Arnold Schwarzenegger in *The Terminator*.

On the basis of chances created, Brazil could have gone in at half-time 4–0 up, but Germany had somehow found the where with all to play like the German teams of 1966, 1982 or 1986 (when they were *worthy* runners-up in England, Spain and Mexico). It really was like watching the great German teams of the past, as they 'won' the first half on points in terms of possession, tactics and corners won. All they lacked was an explosive striker in the mould of Gerd Muller, Karl-Heinz Rummenigge or Jurgen Klinsman. Amazingly Ramelow was playing like Beckenbauer and Schneider like Matthaus. Germany were the superior team, whereas Brazil were performing like a group of individually talented strangers who hadn't been formally introduced. Their four chances were created, almost from nothing, by Ronaldo and Kleberson. The latter clattered the crossbar with a curling shot, while the former was put through on goal as early as the eighth minute by Ronaldhino. Ronaldo's leaden-footed finish with the outside of his boot was ambitious but incompetent, whizzing past the far post by six feet. Twice before half-time he found himself stared down by the advancing Kahn, who blocked both goal-scoring opportunities. Individual Brazilian brilliance was being matched by collective German industry.

In the second half, Germany upped their work-rate and actually went hell-for-leather for the vital opening goal. Neuville lined up a 40-yard free-kick and hit it like Roberto Carlos with a following wind. It was hit so fast and so hard that only replays disclosed Marcos getting fingertips to the ball to deflect it onto the post. Jens Jeremies then had a short-range header cleared off the goal-line by Edmilson. Torsten Frings and Michael Bode had restricted Cafu and Carlos to their own half, with the result that the three Rs were getting almost no service.

In the 68th minute disaster struck, like a lightning bolt sent down by an angry Zeus from his seat upon Mount Olympus (covered in yellow-and-green bunting). Ronaldo fouled Hamman to gain possession but wasn't punished by referee Collina, set up Rivaldo for a quick one-two but kept running when his selfish colleague opted to shoot from distance. Kahn had time to get his body behind the ball as he dived forward to collect the ball in his cradled arms, a save of almost zero technical difficulty. The Fevernova, instead of dying and coming to rest with Kahn clutching it to his chest, somehow bounced off his breast bone into the path of the still-running Ronaldo. The side footed finish was a formality, a gift from the gods wrapped up in a pink ribbon and delivered on a silver platter. Kahn lay sprawled on the grass as if he had just broken his neck (instead of his heart).

The Samba drums burst back into life and despite the cushion of a 1–0 lead Brazil weren't going to rest on their laurels now. Ten minutes later Rivaldo stepped over a cross from the right and Ronaldo pounced to pass the ball into the net. 2–0. When Marcos got a glove to a goal-bound shot from substitute Bierhoff, everyone knew that Germany were beaten.

At some point, I had subconsciously started supporting Germany and when Ronaldo got the first of his brace I remained rooted to my seat. I was surprised that Brazil had taken the lead, but shocked to find that I wasn't celebrating the fact. I actually wanted the Germans to win. Had supporting England up to the quarter-finals somehow screwed up my sense of footballing values? At the final whistle, I felt . . . not gutted, but mildly disappointed. The best team in the tournament had deservedly won, but the best team on the day had unluckily lost.

Kahn sat slumped against a post, eyes closed as he visualised his one error of the competition reverberating into a future where its enormity and importance would become part of footballing folklore. After the 5–1 disaster in Munich, Kahn had commented: 'It was like the explosion of a nuclear bomb. The scars will last for life.' Such hyperbole doesn't leave much room for further comment when even greater misfortune strikes. Kahn had dropped a dreadful brick, which had exploded in his face like a nuclear device. In sport, it doesn't get any worse than this.

Or better, if you happen to be Ronaldo. He declared that the win, combined with the two goals that secured him the Golden Boot with eight strikes, was a mix that was better than sex. The highly sexed, rather than highly sexy, striker then added that: 'I'm going to have sex in a few moments!' In sport, I guess it really doesn't get any better than this. Paris and its consequences – psychological and physical – could have destroyed Ronaldo, but he had been given a second chance and had accepted it gratefully with both feet. Back from the brink of oblivion, he had reached the peak of the mountain – and would never have to look back with an overwhelming sense of regret.

Before the presentation ceremony, the Brazilians got all religious, revealing 'I love Jesus' undershirts and kneeling to pray in a giant circle. Cafu, playing in his third consecutive World Cup final, climbed up on the plinth bearing the trophy and held it aloft as 70,000 supporters acclaimed him. Thousands of origami paper cranes descended on the dias where the Brazilians were waiting to take their turn in holding up the most treasured prize on Planet Football.

Brazil as World Champions was probably the most popular and predictable outcome for this the most entertainingly bizarre of World Cups. There had been no truly great games or toweringly outstanding individuals, but who'd have thought it would have ended with everyone feeling sorry for the Germans?

As hosts in 2006, Germany don't, of course, have to qualify. But for the first time the holders, in this instance Brazil, do. Let's hope they make it there, along with the Republic of Ireland, England and that wonderful little Celtic country currently rated 55th in the world standings – and I don't mean bloody Wales!